# CHANGING LIFESTYLES

Born in 1914, John Seymour is one of the great practical environmentalists of our age. He has spent nearly all his life working on the land and for much of the time he has tried to live as self-sufficiently as possible. At the age of twenty he travelled to Africa in search of adventure and joined the King's African Rifles on the outbreak of war. He saw much active service in Ethiopia and Burma. After the war, and after thirteen years abroad, he returned to England and worked for the Ministry of Agriculture in East Suffolk. Having published the first of his many books in 1953, he began to run a self-sufficient smallholding in Suffolk. Eight years later he moved to a larger one in Pembrokeshire, where he stayed for seventeen years. Ten years ago he passed the land over to his children and moved to Co. Wexford where he lives today. John Seymour has written nearly thirty books, the best-known of which are *The Complete Book of Self Sufficiency* (1976) and, with Herbert Girardet, *Far from Paradise* (1986) and *Blueprint for a Green Planet* (1987).

D1387276

# CHANGING LIFESTYLES

Living as though the world mattered

# JOHN SEYMOUR

LONDON
VICTOR GOLLANCZ LTD
1991

First published in Great Britain 1991
by Victor Gollancz Ltd
14 Henrietta Street, London WC2E 8QJ

A Gollancz Paperback Original

*British Library Cataloguing in Publication Data*
Seymour, John *1914–*
  Changing lifestyles: living as though the world
  mattered.
  1. Environment. Effects of humans
  I. Title
  304.2

ISBN 0-575-04835-2

Typeset at The Spartan Press Ltd,
Lymington, Hants
Printed and bound in Great Britain
by Cox & Wyman Ltd, Reading

# Contents

I wish to express my thanks
to Angela Ashe,
who did much of the research for
this book and without whose help
it would not have been written.

# Introduction

Years ago I wrote a book called *Self Sufficiency*, all about growing your own food. As it was a great success I followed it up with a book called *The Complete Book of Self Sufficiency*.

I began to advocate self sufficiency out of concern for the environment. In 1931, when I went to agricultural college (at Wye in Kent) I was already worried about the way the world was going. I did not like the replacement of agricultural workers by big machines and chemicals; I did not like the way farmers in England were plunging themselves into debt and becoming nothing more than vassals of banks and finance companies; I did not like the way small farms were being swallowed up by big ones, and small fields were being knocked into big ones, and small overdrafts were being made into big ones, and small dole queues were being made into big ones. Also, I was not sure I liked the chemical revolution; it did not seem to be making the smaller farmers richer, which they deserved to be, and I did not think it was good for the soil. I think, even in those days, I had worked out that we humans are soil organisms; we are creatures of the soil, and it behoves us not to abuse it.

After college I went to Africa, and there I roamed for six years. I rode the veld in the Karroo, in South Africa, looking after sheep; I managed a sheep farm in South West Africa (now Namibia) on the verge of the Namib Desert; I shot lions, I hunted buck. I spent a year deep sea fishing, six months down a copper mine in what is now called Zambia, and a couple of years, or so, roaming the bush of central Africa, inoculating native cattle.

I admired the way tribal Africans lived; I liked how they had come to terms with their environment. I felt that if they could only be left alone they would go on living in harmony with the world around them. But they were not left alone; the Arab slave traders had not left them alone and the new colonial powers would not leave them alone either. They were forced into a money economy, and taxes were imposed on them which they had to pay in cash (a thing they had hitherto known nothing of). To earn the tax money the young men were forced to go to the Copperbelt – or the Rand – and work in the mines. I also spent some time in Ethiopia; the land – high, cool and rainy – was the most fertile I had encountered in Africa and certainly the best farmed. If you had told me that forty years of extractive mechanized farming would destroy for ever that wonderful fertile soil, and render the most prosperous peasantry in Africa destitute, I would have laughed at you.

## The History of Change

One of the best friends I ever had was a man of the Old Stone Age. White people unable to get their tongues round his real name, which was a conglomeration of clicks, called him Joseph. He was a Bushman, or *Koi-san* person, of the Namib Desert in South West Africa, but he had been caught by a white farmer and made to work as a child and had therefore learnt Afrikaans; as I knew a smattering of this language I could communicate with him. He worked as a shepherd on my boss's farm.

I used to go hunting with him. At first he would hand his flock of sheep over to his wife and we would walk out into the bush to search for *gemsbok*, or oryx, which were very common in those days. Joseph had what seemed to me to be an uncanny knack of knowing where they were. When he knew me better, he asked me to leave my rifle behind and he used to put his arm into a thorn bush and pull out from it the head of a spear. It was quite illegal for a 'native' in South West Africa to own a spear, or any other weapon, so he kept it hidden. He would fit the spearhead to a shaft, which he cut from the bush, borrow three of his neighbours' dogs, and off we would go. The dogs would bring a buck to bay and Joseph would kill it with his spear.

Once Joseph took leave, and he and I trekked north to the Otasha Pan, where he introduced me to his 'wild' relations, and we stayed with them a few days. Although they, or their ancestors, had been driven by the advancing Bantu Africans into the most desolate and inhospitable part of Africa, they still managed to live very well. They hunted very successfully – not with the spear and dogs as Joseph and I did – but by lying near waterholes or salt licks with a bow and little poisoned arrow. How the first Bushman discovered that by mixing the juice of a certain beetle with that of a certain desert plant you got a deadly poison I cannot imagine, but one did.

In that dry wilderness they could find water by cutting open the stomach of a *gemsbok* and drinking the contents, as I learnt to do myself. Or they would find an insignificant-looking creeper, dig down under it, and bring up a soggy mass of vegetation as big as a football.

Out of this they would suck water and very nasty it tasted too, but very welcome when it could keep you alive.

They did no work. They could walk forty miles in a night. They would wait patiently for hour after hour by a waterhole for a buck. The women dug up edible corms or bulbs from the *veld* with *gemsbok* horns, but meat was the staple diet. When they killed a buck they would gorge, grilling the meat on the hot ashes of the fire, eating every part of the animal – even cracking the bones to get at the marrow. I know all this, not because I read it in a book of anthropology but because I joined in – I was there.

Life was hard as the climate was very uncomfortable – roasting hot as soon as the sun got up in the morning, and very cold at night. They spent most nights dancing and singing and telling stories in the light of their fires. They were completely at home with the natural world around them; they knew every being in it, whether animal, vegetable or rock. They never felt, for one moment, that they were in any way special, or apart from the rest of Nature.

I moved to Central Africa and there, in the country now called Zambia, worked and lived among people of the New Stone Age. True, they had iron and steel implements which they had traded from Europeans but, in their culture and way of life, they were Neolithic – of the New Stone Age. They were herdsmen and cultivators. In Barotseland, which was a kingdom in the headwaters country of the Zambesi River, the boys herded cattle in the open bush, while the men (whose symbolic emblem was an axe) felled forest trees and burnt the wood. The women (whose symbol was the hoe) then moved in, hoed the partially-cleared ground, and planted millet, maize, sorghum, sweet potatoes and other crops. The men hunted, not very successfully, milked the cows, occasionally slaughtered an ox (only for special occasions) and searched for wild honey. The men and boys fished in the rivers with nets; the women fished in shallow waters with baskets. The women pounded the corn in mortars, cooked, and brewed beer. People of both sexes built new huts when required; it took a day to build a living hut and most comfortable dwellings they were. I know – I spent months in them.

I tell all this because I want to point out the enormous *change of lifestyle* people underwent with the Neolithic – or agricultural – revolution. For nearly all of human history humans lived like my Bushman friends did. They knew their environment so intimately that they could find their food in it without really working. They toiled not neither did they spin. They made no impact on their environment either for good or for ill. They never seriously depleted the stocks of the wild animals they hunted. They did not keep grazing animals and allow them to overgraze. They did not dig or plough and cause erosion. They did not cut down trees. (There is evidence that in some cases – certainly in Australia – fires they started in the bush to drive wild animals changed the vegetation of the country. My own belief is that this was exceptional.)

Suddenly, only perhaps ten or twelve thousand years ago, people discovered they could plant seed and reap crops, and also – just as important – tame and domesticate wild animals. There was an enormous change in lifestyle; to the participants it must have seemed absolutely earth-shattering.

Suddenly people had to stay in one place, they could no longer roam; and they had to *work*. Without hard and consistent work you cannot grow, harvest, store and process crops for food. Suddenly they had to learn how to build permanent buildings. They found they had more *security* than people had ever had before; they could store up food. Populations began to increase and pushed against the supply of cultivable land, and so wars began. War became a constant factor in human affairs. All the great Bronze Age epics, such as the Irish *Tain*, the Greek Homeric epics, the Indian *Ramayana* and *Mahabharata*, the Hebrew Old Testament, speak of war and more war. Whereas Joseph's brethren owned practically nothing and had nothing to fight about, the agricultural revolution, enabling humans to store food and occupy land, also gave them something to go to war about, and so to war they did.

Many things resulted from this revolution: cities, king-craft and priestcraft, literature, art – all that we now call civilization. We made that great change in lifestyle in the past, and now we are a farming species – and if we are to have a future it is that. We cannot become hunter-gatherers again, like my friend Joseph's brethren. We wouldn't know how. We have changed – and degraded – the natural world too much for it to be able to support us. Anyway there are too many of us. I know many advocates of a return to hunter-gatherer economics. They mostly live in London, drive large cars, and wouldn't know how to snare a rabbit. No, we are farmers now, for good or for evil. The most trendy and urbanized punk rocker in the middle of London or New York is a farming animal, entirely dependent for his or her life, all of it, upon the farm and the farmer.

The change from hunting to farming might have been quite benign as far as the life of this planet was concerned. The farmer takes a piece of the Earth's surface and reduces the number of species of living things on it but may well increase the *biomass*, i.e. the actual bulk or weight of living matter that it produces. The farmer may also increase the fertility of that piece of land. The farming lifestyle *could* be sustainable – as long as this world lasts.

## The Industrial Revolution

I envy the first farmers. They had security, for the first time in human history, they had hard work but it was healthy hard work, they 'ate their bread in the sweat of their brow' but enjoyed it all the more for it, and as long as they were left alone by other people they could be happy and content. Unfortunately they were seldom left alone. Conquerors almost always came, and taxed them, and took their land and made them pay rents for it, and conscripted them into armies and sent them to war. In most parts of the world, for most of human history since farming began, the farmer has been grossly exploited by city people, as is still the case in most places today.

The coming of the Industrial Revolution in the Western world led to another huge change in lifestyles, as millions left the land and swarmed into the new cities. People said that city air was free air, and indeed it must have seemed like that to landless labourers escaping from lives of toil and poverty, and subservience to the local squire; but they soon found that freedom also included freedom to starve. The very technologies that sucked people into the cities also drove labourers from the land, because they replaced the labour of people with machines. The horse-drawn reaper and the threshing machine alone put thousands of country people out of work.

The Industrial Revolution caused the most drastic

changes in lifestyles since the beginning of farming. It turned the majority of mankind into machine-minders. It destroyed the dignity of labour, and the joy of creativeness; it condemned millions to live in horrible conditions, in city slums. It also began the assault on the life-systems of this planet, and if it continues unchecked will undoubtedly destroy it—or at least the life that is on it, including our own.

Now we are in the midst of the Technological Revolution and this, again, is bringing about great changes in lifestyles. It is bringing great material prosperity to a few: the people who have, as one might say, their hands on the electronic levers of power. One person can sit in an air-conditioned office and, by pressing a few keys or speaking a few times into a telephone, gain many thousands of pounds. Another can work down a mine winning a hundred tons of coal, at risk to life, and make a paltry few pounds. The price of dwellings for humans goes sky-high and the cardboard cities, the shanty-towns of the homeless, spread. The farmers and farm-workers – the members of the tiny dwindling army that has to feed the lot of us, have to cope with bigger and bigger areas of cropland, often working hours that would not be considered possible by any city person, and being forced to adopt methods which many of the farmers themselves, in their hearts, know are damaging to the land.

After the Second World War I spent a year in India and hated what I saw there – for I could see that the *soil* was going. There were commercial loggers going up into the forests and clear-felling them all, and as soon as the trees went the soil went – down the slopes and into the Ganges, the Bhramaputra and the Godavari, and on into the sea. There were hoards of 'community project' officers from the United States going around trying to make people sell their milk and other produce so that they could get money to spend on foreign imported goods; In other words getting the Indian peasant hooked into the money economy.

Gandhi's disciples were resisting movement into large-scale commerce; their policy was one of village self-sufficiency, but I could see that they were not going to be heeded. India was going to fall holus-bolus into the maelstrom of materialism and commercialism-gone-mad. The village in which I spent a month in the Punjab was having pressure put on it to go for the so-called 'green revolution'. One *ryot* (farmer) had already gone in for it. He had borrowed money – more money than that whole village had ever imagined could exist – and bought a tractor. He had allowed aid workers from the United States to supply him with the new short-strawed high-yielding but very disease-prone and pest-prone wheat. This wheat would only grow if copiously dressed with artificial manure, so he was having to go further into debt to buy that; then the growing crop had to be sprayed constantly to keep it alive – and this meant further debt.

But the banks loved the 'green revolution'. They love people going into debt, and hate them getting out of it. The manufacturers of shoddy 'high-tech' goods, whether in the United States, Japan or Europe, loved it too; they had a new market. As for the soil of that great plain – it could not stand up to tractor-and-chemical cultivation and was going down the Ganges into the sea.

## The Alternative

When I came back to England, I rented a little piece of land in Suffolk, and really became 'self sufficient'. I just tried to opt out of what William Cobbett called 'the Thing' – frenetic urban life. I had a family, which grew to six, and we did the best we could. Somehow we kind of blundered into the situation where we were producing nearly everything we required from our five acres of rented sandy land near the Suffolk coast. We didn't grow wheat but bought our flour from a still-existing windmill at Friston. We bought a little stock-food from the watermill at Wickham Market. We certainly more than paid for it with the sale of weaner pigs, for our six sows used to produce a hundred and twenty piglets a year with monotonous regularity. We fattened and killed first one, and then – as the children grew up and ate more – three baconers a year, and made our own bacon, ham, sausages, and all the rest of it. We had a cow, who became one of the family, and we had all our own milk, cheese, butter – as much as we could ever consume. As we had no deep freeze we didn't kill our own beef but sold a big calf a year and bought beef with the money. The cow and the pigs gave us abounding fertility and our five sandy acres grew a huge amount of vegetables, grass, hay, pig food and whatever we or our animals and poultry required. We had a horse for ploughing – and for pulling our governess cart, because for years we did not have a motor. We were fine, fit and happy and the doctor never had to come down our long sandy lane.

We moved to Wales and lived the same way there, only more so, and on more land. We grew wheat, barley and oats too, and brewed our own beer. We had a boat and caught our own seafish. We sheared our own sheep and spun some of the wool and my wife knitted and wove. We even produced, pulled, retted, broke, scutched and spun our own *flax*!

You may say – 'we can't *all* live like that'. No – we

cannot all live like that, but what we *can* all attempt – and must all aim towards – is a much greater measure of regional self-sufficiency.

We have always been taught to welcome anything that is 'good for trade'. We must get out of this way of thinking – it is too *much* trade that is destroying our planet; we simply do not need so much. The more we lug stuff backwards and forwards across the face of this suffering Earth the more harm we do to her. Within living memory the village in Suffolk near where I lived for eight years had: a corn-miller, a blacksmith and farrier, a wheelwright, a carpenter-cum-undertaker, a butcher who killed his own animals, a dress-maker, a tailor, half a dozen fishermen, an ironmonger, several builders, and a maltings and a brewery. Now it has none of these things, not one. If you want anything that you cannot produce yourself you have to go many miles for it. Foolish people say to me 'That's progress!' No doubt, but it is progress in the *wrong direction*.

In Britain we are being told we are all 'going into Europe' in 1992; everything we use or consume will come to us from hundreds of miles away. *Nothing* will be local any more. Well *I* am not 'going into Europe'! I will buy good French, or other European wine, as I do now, for little wine is produced in the country where I live. 'Country' wines, yes, we make them here – but the juice of the grape – not much. Therefore it is legitimate to trade with other countries for wine. For tea and coffee perhaps too. But for very little else. If we don't have enough hard wood timber, then we should damned well plant some trees.

We have created lifestyles which are not sustainable, and the forces of destruction being turned against our living planet gain momentum all the time. Even our politicians (the last people ever to become aware of anything) are beginning to wake up to the facts.

Changes in human lifestyle accelerate all the time. Old Stone Age Man, the hunter and gatherer, went on almost exactly the same for two million years. The Neolithic period lasted a piddling eight thousand years before it gave way to the Bronze Age. The Iron Age might be said to have lasted a thousand years, the Age of the Internal Combustion Engine will only have lasted a hundred and fifty before we run out of oil. Human history is moving at a greater and increasing speed. The next great turning point will come astonishingly soon: in the lifetimes of most of us who are here now. Surely it is better to change sensibly, the way we want to, to our own plan, than to have it forced upon us. In the latter case, the change will be violent, destructive and very, very difficult to cope with.

In the following pages I put forward, humbly I hope, a few suggestions as to how we may make the necessary adjustment ourselves and not wait for the apocalypse. I have chosen some individual aspects of our present way of living to illustrate both the need for change and the possibilities of doing so. I do not ask you to follow my suggestions, merely to consider them.

# ENERGY

# 1. The Question of Energy

There is an organization in Wales called the Saint David's Forum, which convenes a symposium every year on some important subject. One year I was invited to attend it; the subject was *Energy*.

The public relations officer for the nuclear power industry was there, and he was putting the case for nuclear power with the help of one of those little instruments that projects an image up onto a screen. His case rested on a frightening graph representing the world's energy requirements from the year 1800 to the present day. The curve representing energy requirements started in 1800 at near zero, rose throughout the industrial revolution, took a bad jerk upward in the First World War, an even worse one in the Second World War, and then went on rising in an ever-steepening curve to the present day. What he had not noticed was that there was a big illuminated sign which said 'EXIT' on the wall exactly in line with his projection.

Surely every thoughtful person in the world realizes that we cannot continue projecting that curve upward and upward for ever and ever without coming, in very truth, to 'exit' for humankind. What? – every family in the USSR (population 267 million), in India (population 683 million), China (a thousand million) to have a motor car to pump out $CO_2$ and a deep-freeze to destroy the ozone layer? And a colour television, and a video machine, and central heating, and air conditioning, and a plastic 'yacht' on a trailer in the front drive, and, and . . . ? But we of the wealthy West have all of these things. Why shouldn't they? After all they can all have catalytic converters in their exhaust pipes. They can fit scrubbers to their power station chimneys. China alone is planning to have a thousand new coal-fired power stations during the next decade. A *thousand*! All churning out carbon dioxide into the atmosphere (no scrubbers can stop that – if you burn hydrocarbon you get $CO_2$). All adding to the pollution of our planet's atmosphere, seas, rivers and lakes. And the whole world to be covered with plastic factories producing PVCs, and dioxin, and other persistent poisons, and fertilizer factories to turn out more and more nitrate to pollute the water systems, and pesticide factories, and all the other factories to bring the entire world population up to the 'standard of living' of the inhabitants of Dallas, U.S.A., or at least of Dallas as it exists on the television screen and the imaginations of millions?

Surely a moment's reflection is enough to persuade any sensible person that *this is not going to happen*. Not only are the billions of the 'Third World' not going to achieve the 'Dallas standard' but the inhabitants of Dallas are not going to maintain it much longer either. For, given the Earth's resources, and her capacity to absorb our wastes, it is not sustainable.

At that Saint David's Forum, where the nuclear apologist projected his line so unfortunately at the word 'EXIT', every conceivable source of energy, as applied to human needs and uses, was discussed by experts, in detail, except the most widespread and useful of all: the energy produced by human muscle. I was the only one to mention that particular sort of energy – at the after-dinner speech at the end of the conference.

For millions of years that source of energy was not only the most important one, but the only one, for *Homo sapiens*. For millions of people living on this planet today, it still is. But in various parts of the world, and in various ages, we tamed the ass and the horse, the ox and the yak, the llama and the buffalo, and augmented our feebler muscles with theirs. Then we found that falling water and wind could be made to do some of our more boring and repetitive work like grinding corn, and that the wind could drive our ships on the sea. The invention of sailing into the wind – tacking – was a tremendous breakthrough, and allowed world travel and exploration.

But all the time, without knowing it, we were walking about on top of enormous reserves of stored energy. For thousands of years we had warmed ourselves and our dwellings, and cooked our food, by burning wood, and peat which had providentially formed in countries short of trees; but it was not until the late Middle Ages that coal began to be used as a fuel, where it outcropped at first, and subsequently underground. Eventually, inevitably, we learned to turn its latent energy into motion. Then came oil, and that proved beyond any comparison to be the most 'efficient' source of energy we had ever discovered.

I was born in 1914, and at that time the exploitation of oil was in its infancy. The industrial world was still coal-powered. The oil boom had only just begun in the western United States; the huge reserves of oil in the Middle East, and other parts of the globe, had not been discovered. Very very few people drove motor cars in 1914. My mother drove a Studebaker and was considered amazing for doing so; women drivers were very rare indeed. None of the roads in our part of Essex were tarred and there were far more horse-drawn vehicles than motor ones. If I live to be

a hundred I believe I will have seen the oil-age, substantially, right through from its start to its finish.

Oh I know there were motor cars in the 1890s but they
were objects of wonder, not a serious means of getting
about. And I suspect there will be some petrol or diesel-
driven motor cars about in 2014, but they too, I believe,
will be rare enough to be objects of wonder; for by then the
petroleum that will power them will be a scarce commod-
ity, and very few people will be able to afford it. Oh yes –
people will continue to find more reserves of oil, maybe for
centuries to come, but under deeper and deeper oceans,
and more inaccessible places; we are already beginning to
scrape the bottom of the barrel.

Consider this: as the fuel derived from oil gets scarcer
and more expensive, it will cost more and more to look for
oil and to transport it, as this process itself demands huge
amounts of fuel. Similarly, it will become more expensive
to build things like nuclear power stations, or coal-fired
ones either for that matter. For it is *oil* that gives us the
apparently boundless power to do whatever we feel we
want to do. There will be other sources of energy, no
doubt, and coal may last for several hundred years in some
quantity of supply; but *nothing* will ever give us the power
of a liquid which comes bubbling out of the ground
whenever anyone drills a hole in the right place. Petroleum
stands quite apart from any other source of energy,
renewable or non-renewable, because of its extreme
availability. Nobody has to go underground to get it, it can
be transported extremely cheaply with pipe lines or super
tankers (it does not have to be loaded into the holds of
ships and grabbed out again), nobody ever has to touch it
or heave it about: its transportation involves nothing more
than the turning on or off of a few taps. Methane gas, of

course, has many of the same advantages, although it is less cheap to transport it in tankers or road transport, for it then has to be compressed or frozen in some way. Oil just flows.

However, we don't need to use up our oil supplies (or gas or coal ones either for that matter) at anything like the rate at which we are using them up. If we humans knew what our real interests were we would begin right now the effort to phase out the use of oil – and coal – just as fast as we can. This is for several reasons, by far the most important being to reduce the emission of carbon dioxide.

The atmosphere of the world before the Carboniferous Age (which lasted from about 320 to 270 million years ago) was heavily loaded with carbon dioxide gas ($CO_2$). Members of the animal kingdom need plenty of free oxygen, of which there was little, because most of the O was tied up as $CO_2$. But members of the vegetable kingdom require $CO_2$ – they tie up the carbon part of it in their tissue and release the oxygen as free oxygen.

The world was like a vast greenhouse, very humid and hot (because of the prevalence of 'greenhouse gases' in the atmosphere) and with a carbon-laden atmosphere very favourable to the growth of plants (modern growers sometimes generate $CO_2$ in their greenhouses). So the plant kingdom proliferated to such an extent that the mass of dead vegetation it generated was unable to rot, and instead was turned into peat, coal and oil. These latter, together with the vast biomass of the living vegetable kingdom, locked up huge quantities of carbon and so left the oxygen in the air as free oxygen which enabled the animal kingdom to expand and evolve larger and more complex species.

Now it is quite obvious that if we burn up all the fossil

fuels produced at that time, thus releasing all the carbon they contain back into the air, and also burn up the forests, which are needed to lock up vast amounts of carbon, we are going to return to a world favourable to plants and unfavourable to us and other animals. Maybe, in cosmic terms, this would be a good thing. We animals would mostly die out (a few simple creatures with very slow metabolic rates would presumably survive the anoxic conditions), the plant kingdom would burgeon, another Carboniferous age would result and the whole cycle would begin again. Maybe *next* time round the first animal to be evolved with an analytical intelligence would have the sense not to screw it all up again. Who knows?

But meanwhile I feel I have a vested interest in the status quo. I am an animal and I want to go on being an animal, and I want my children – and their children – to continue to exist. We humans have already affected the chemistry of the air to a massive extent during the couple of hundred years in which we have been burning fossil fuels and substantially destroying the forests. At last, if only during the last couple of years, our climatologists are *quite sure* that we are altering the climate. This change can only go on happening at an ever-accelerating rate: there are so many positive feedbacks involved. There are sober and cautious scientists about who are telling us that we may be on the brink of disaster.

If we really knew what our interests were we would start to phase out fossil-fuel burning *now* – and stop destroying the forests too, immediately. Tentative palliative measures will simply not be effective. Every year that we put off positive action is a year too long. Why, you may say, can we not leave this to politicians? After all they have grandchildren too and they can take effective action because they have the power. But the overriding interest of every politician in the world is to secure election. A politician won't do that by doubling the price of, say, electricity; so we non-politicians have got to do the job ourselves. Put pressure on our politicians by all means; voting 'Green' can only do good. But in the end each one of us has got to take responsibility for what we do, and what we don't do. There is only one person in the universe over whose actions I have complete control and that is myself.

Here we come bang up against the phenomenon of the 'Tragedy of the Commons'. What possible difference to the future of the world will it make if *I* walk up the office stairs instead of riding in the lift while everyone else still takes the lift? Or switch the heating down and put another pullover on, or buy locally-produced goods instead of goods from far away, or don't drive around in a car so much, if everyone else just carries on as before? We all have these thoughts, and so each one of us goes on acting as if there will be no tomorrow; which there won't be if we don't change our ways. But if it is true that the only person over whose actions I have control is myself – then *it does matter what I do*. It may not matter a jot to 'the world', or to 'life', or to the person nearest, but it must matter to *me*. So, if there is to be any hope for us, each one of us must take responsibility for what we do.

There is, by good fortune, one factor that could help us to achieve all this. To use the power that our muscles give us is not only good for the planet but good for us. Our bodies are meant to be worked hard and if they are not worked hard they will deteriorate. *Laziness* was bred into the human race by the forces of natural selection, for our hunting ancestors had far too much physical exercise to take and therefore it was essential that they should have the urge to rest when they could rest. But now we have far too little need for exercise – and yet the bred-in urge to rest is still with us, and we wish to rest far more than we should for the good of our bodies.

We should walk, or cycle, to work far more than we do. I find I can walk from one point to another in inner London nearly as quickly as another person can go by public transport. We should walk up the stairs instead of going in the lift. Not only will that spare electrical power but it will do us good. Lifts are a wonderful invention for the disabled, but are mostly used by the able-bodied. We should make use, whenever we can, of that first and most widespread machine for turning latent energy into work: the human muscle. When a country person is splitting logs a neighbour is sure to come along and say 'It warms you twice!' It probably warms the one taking exercise many more times than that before it gets onto the fire.

It is commonly said that the course of action that would cut down most on consumption of fossil fuel would be to *save* more energy. We should insulate our houses far better, wear more clothes, be more physically active (it is the sedentary person who requires a temperature like that of a hot-house), fit more efficient heating systems, drive more fuel-efficient cars or no cars at all, use more public transport. There are various estimates, or wild guesses, and most of them indicate that we could save 50 per cent of the energy produced by fossil fuels in such ways. Well, if we could achieve that, it might put off global cataclysm for several decades. Surely we should all go all out for it? If the governments of this world had spent a hundredth part of the money they have spent on developing nuclear power on energy-saving devices the world would be in a far better state than it is. And this is something we could all do. If every one of us resolved to cut our use of energy produced by fossil fuels by half, what an enormous difference it would make. And how much fitter and happier we would all be!

The advocates of nuclear power have a very simple answer to the whole problem. The French have the policy: *tout électrique tout nucléaire*. Since Chernobyl they have not been quite so enthusiastic about singing that song, although it is noteworthy that the radioactivity of that disaster, although it was detected in some strength right along the German side of the French-German frontier, proved quite unable to cross to France! Not one rem could be discovered by French investigators on their side of the border, which either tells us something about the efficiency of the German geiger counters or about the honesty of the French government.

But, the French apart, it is obvious that nuclear energy is not going to prove the solution to our energy problems. The fact that no private investors, anywhere in the world, are willing to invest a penny in it is evidence enough. Even when the British government agreed to pay *all* waste disposal costs, plus decommissioning costs, plus the cost of further research and development, when trying to flog off the nuclear industry, even *then* the City of London would not invest one penny in it. But by the year 2025, even if no more reactors are built, five hundred and five reactors will have to be decommissioned worldwide, and the estimate for the cost of decommissioning each one stood at three billion US dollars back in 1986 – what it will be by 2025 beggars the imagination! The cost of decommissioning will be far far higher than the cost of building. And the disposal of the resulting radioactive waste will poison a substantial part of our planet however we do it; we are leaving a frightful problem for our grandchildren. It would be criminal to saddle posterity with more of this sort of problem by building more reactors. Governments may go on building them to satisfy their apparently insatiable appetite for plutonium for bombs but there can be *no* economic reason. Our politicians may take the attitude that 'It won't matter what our descendants think of us because we will be dead then!' Well, if we take that attitude we deserve to become extinct; the world will be well rid of us.

So I'm afraid that nuclear is no solution. What was to be the ultimate in free lunches does not really work. We are left though with plenty of alternatives, and we will discuss some of these in the next chapter.

## 2. Benign Sources of Energy

We have discussed the most benign and least harmful of all: human muscle. But there are plenty of others. The Sun pours enough energy on to this planet every day to heat all the houses and power all the machines that we could ever possibly require. The Sun causes winds to blow, waves to surge, rain to fall, rivers to flow, 'biomass' to grow.

I know a young couple in North Wales who have a tiny windmill (a 'Rutland', for which they paid £200) and a photovoltaic panel which uses sunlight directly to generate electricity and which cost them £150; these two pieces of equipment give them all the electric light they need right throughout the year. They do not have enough power to work a washing machine, and certainly not an electric fire, but electricity is especially suited for certain things, and surely lighting is the first of them? I lived for eight years on a smallholding in Suffolk with no electricity, and had none where I live now in Ireland for a long time and got on pretty well without it. But I have to admit paraffin lighting is far more expensive than electricity and a damn site more messy. It was marvellous on both occasions when the power was switched on to be able to give up the chore of cleaning, and lighting, paraffin pressure lamps every day. Adequate lighting uses very little electrical current, and the new economical bulbs make it even more economic. Of course we should not forget that we *could* make use of a lot more daylight and therefore need less lighting; early to bed and early to rise saves energy besides making us healthy, wealthy and wise!

Driving small machines is another very good use for electrical current. I am old enough to remember factories in England where people used to work amidst a forest of whipping belts carrying power from whirring shafts overhead to numerous machines below, while a huge old steam engine puffed and panted in a separate room at one end of the factory. The replacement of all those belts by safe and inconspicuous electric cables must have been seen as a good thing.

Electricity for heating, even for cooking, is another matter though. As long as the electricity comes from fossil-fuel burning we should avoid it, for only a small percentage of the energy provided by burning the fuel ends up by heating our fire. But it is the provenance of electrical power that is everything. If the power comes from benign renewable sources, and in sufficient quantity, then surely it doesn't matter so much how 'efficient' electricity is?

People who want to sell us electricity or electrical applicances are always telling us how *clean* it is. And indeed in our kitchens it creates no smoke, no fumes. The smoke and fumes are there all right but unless we live near a power station we don't see them. It is quite obvious what we have got to do about electricity – we have got to use far less of it and we have got to generate far more of it with renewable energy sources.

It is a global scandal that so little has been done about developing wind power. The principles of generating electricity from the wind are well understood – there are successful applications all around the world – and yet the expansion is woefully slow. This is *not* due to the cost or ineffectiveness of it. I do not normally believe in conspiracy theories – people are generally too stupid and disunited for that – but here I do suspect a conspiracy, or something very like it. Centralized government fears decentralization, particularly when it comes to such an important thing as energy production. The Central Electricity Generating Board in England and Wales closed down all the small hydro-electric power stations: not because they were producing expensively but because the Board claimed they were too scattered – too hard to administer. I am suspicious, *a priori*, of any research done by the C.E.G.B. into renewable energy sources; it is biased against them from the beginning.

And there has been a subtle whispering campaign against wind power. All sorts of strange rumours have been put about. For example it is claimed that wind generators are abominably noisy! Well the other day I stood within fifty yards of the biggest wind generator in the British Isles – on the Orkney Islands – in a gale, and could hardly hear it. Just a gentle whooshing sound – quite pleasant. I would rather live fifty yards from that than fifty miles from a nuclear power station. Wind generators are supposed to be ugly! They are not: they are among the most beautiful objects mankind has so far devised on this planet. And in any case, if they seem ugly to you – are they as ugly as a nuclear reprocessing plant? Or a uranium mine? Which would you rather: a lot of practically silent windmills spinning away on hill tops; or a climate altered for ever by $CO_2$ emission, the protective ozone layer destroyed, and our fossel fuel deposits burnt up in a generation?

Popular pressure has forced electricity utilities in certain countries to be open to buying electricity from private producers. Now it is natural that they should wish to pay

less for the stuff than they sell it for: that is fair trading and
they have got to install and maintain the grid. But so far
their buying-in prices have been derisory. These prices
should, of course, be set by an independent tribunal. But
even with these derisory prices wind power is doing quite
well. In California investment in 'wind farms' gives a very
good return on capital. If all electrical utilities were
obliged by law to buy wind-generated electricity, and pay
a fair price for it, *and* if planning authorities were forced
to permit the construction of windmills, a big windmill-
making industry would grow up, the capital costs of wind
turbines would plummet, and windmills and wind farms
would spring up all over the world. No more fossil-fuel-
burning power stations would be built, some of the
existing ones would be closed down. The potential for
wind power is immense – it is as big as the sky.

The centralists try to destroy the case for all alternatives
by demolishing them one by one. We should not be
misled by this. They claim wind power is no good because
the wind does not always blow. The answer to that is: no,
but it does sometimes. They say solar power is no good
because the sun does not always shine. No, but it does
sometimes. Tidal power is no good because there are slack
tides every six hours? Yes, but the tide does flow in
between these times. Hydro power is no good because
rivers sometimes run low? Yes, but they don't always.
Geothermal power is no good because you can't get it
everywhere? Yes, but you can get it in *some* places, so get it
there. Wave power is no good because the sea is sometimes
calm? Yes, but it isn't always.

In other words, we must get out of the compartmental-
ized way of thinking. We should develop *all* these renewable resources. When the wind isn't blowing in one place it

is blowing somewhere else! And even if it were not blowing anywhere there would be water falling, or tides ebbing and flowing, or pumped storage schemes operating, and if the worst came to the worst then we could fall back on fossil fuel for just the time of shortage.

If engineers and industrialists could only be persuaded to take the issue of fossil-fuel burning seriously, research and development would go ahead in great bounds. For example, there are ways of storing energy which have hardly been developed. Windmills and other devices go on producing at night as well as by day, but it is in the day that the power is required. Storage batteries for electricity seem to have intrinsic limitations, but you can use electrical current to split water – thus releasing the oxygen and obtaining hydrogen. With the latter you can drive cars and other engines. The product of burning hydrogen is entirely harmless: just water vapour. Not a trace of carbon. Cars have been very successfully adapted to run off hydrogen, but it almost seems as if the oil mafia will do anything to thwart such developments.

Photovoltaics, the production of electricity from direct sunlight, has enormous potential. It could well be this, and this alone – after more development – which supplies the bulk of the world's energy needs. After all nobody can claim that there is ever a day when the Sun does not shine upon our Earth, and if it is not shining on one side of it then it is shining on the other. The linking up of national grids could spread this power to where it is needed.

Further, photovoltaics lends itself marvellously to decentralization. Homesteads and villages far from any electricity grid can have the benefits of electrical power with its use. If photovoltaic cells become cheap enough every house in the world could have a solar panel somewhere and provide at least some of its energy from this source. Large-scale plants are also feasible. A Sacramento city utility is constructing a unit which will provide a hundred megawatts of power when it comes on stream in 1994.

An apparent anomaly is the current investment by the big oil companies in photovoltaics. At heart they have an ambivalent attitude towards it – and other sources of renewable power. In the first place the oil companies make their money from selling *oil* – and they look upon any other power source as a competitor. But also they have the bleak knowledge that their stock-in-trade is rapidly running out. Therefore they want to invest in renewables so that they can survive in the future. Their attitude seems to be that they want to invest in them, but then keep them under wraps until they have extracted and sold all the oil, for it is the oil that makes the big money.

But oil tycoons have grandchildren too. And they are presumably intelligent enough to heed the warnings of the world's scientists. Is it too much to expect of their intelligence – and far-sightedness – that they should change their strategies entirely, go all out for alternative sources of energy, and conserve the oil reserves of this planet as long as possible? With the kind of money they could put into it they could cover the world with windmills, and photovoltaic cells, and all the rest of it – and conserve the remaining reserves of what made them wealthy in the first place.

We humans are all inhabitants of this planet. And no matter how rich and powerful we may be we are entirely dependent on the planet's life-support systems working properly, to produce clean air, clean water, good soil and to ensure the survival of forests. Is it too much to ask that the powers that rule over us should accept the deadly seriousness of the problems that face us and make an all-out effort, first to cut down on energy requirements, and second to produce such energy as we need from benign sources? It could be done, within the next decade, if the will were there.

The energy problem is easier to solve for we who live in the country than for those who live in the city. The latter can really only put pressure on the authorities, and try to save energy as much as possible; we country bumpkins can to a certain extent help solve our own problems.

There is a steady increase in the number of very small hydro-electric plants in the hilly areas. We do not hear much about these. The government does all it can to discourage such enterprises – like allowing the water boards to charge for the water they 'use', although in fact they don't use the water at all – they merely borrow it for a few minutes and then put it back again. But Nanny doesn't like the children to be too independent! As small windmills become cheaper many more will be installed by country people. To have one simply coupled to a storage heater in the house would drastically cut down on power require-ments from the grid.

But it must not be thought that it is always necessary to use energy-machines to produce electricity and then turn the electricity back into energy again; there is always a loss in doing this. The cheap and simple water-heating solar panel is a marvellous device. I have a friend who construc-ted his own from some old radiators and his bath water is too hot to put your hand in in the summer and at least has the chill off it on many days in mid-winter. When it is not hot enough he boosts it with electricity, and as the water has been pre-warmed this is very cheap. If he had a wind generator as well he could couple this direct to the immersion heater and cut out even more of the mains electricity.

Being completely untechnical, very hard-up, and terribly busy (or at least terribly *lazy* perhaps) I have managed to install none of these things, but I do have my driftwood. I live near the bank of a huge tidal river and we run our central-heating stove almost entirely on driftwood that we haul out of it. *Most* of the year we have a warm house, boiling water, and a hot oven for the cost of sweat alone, and we do not have to fell a tree to do it.

The felling of trees for burning is not, as it happens, as bad as it sounds. In fact it is quite benign. If you clear-fell a wood, or a forest, and burn the timber, you are contributing massively to the greenhouse effect and all the other nasty things that are happening to our planet. But if you plant a new woodland, harvest the timber as it becomes ready, and burn it, you are actually helping to *prevent* the greenhouse effect. The reason is this: the wood, as it is standing, acts as a carbon sink and locks up carbon from the air where it would do harm. When the trees become old they cease to grow very fast and stop locking up so much carbon. When we burn the old trees we do release carbon into the air – BUT we also cause other younger, more vigorous, trees to grow, and these take up carbon more quickly than the old trees. So if we plant a wood where no wood was before, *even* though we burn mature trees we are helping our old planet by locking some carbon up out of the air. And if we turn the timber into furniture, or bulding material, we are doing even better in this respect, for the wood will not release its carbon until it either rots or catches fire. There is *nothing* a man or a woman can do in the world today more beneficial than planting trees.

So to sum it all up, what can the ordinary citizen *do* to help save fossil fuel and thereby help to save our planet? Well first and foremost use far less of it. Use less electricity, less coal and gas. A one-off expenditure on better insulation will result in years – maybe hundreds of years – of energy economy. Second put pressure on governments, on local authorities, on industry, to favour any project which will slow down the burning of fossil fuel. That ever-steepening curve of energy use that my nuclear apologist drew on his screen must be brought to an abrupt halt, *and* be made to come screaming down again. We must press for more and faster development of renewable energy sources all the time. If we have spare money to invest we should invest it in wind power, water power, solar power and anything that gives us useful energy without burning fossil fuel.

Conservationists must always support projects designed to reduce the use of fossil fuels. I remember sitting in the house of a lady who considered she was a great conservationist objecting to the environmental effects of building a pumped-storage scheme near her holiday house in North Wales. The scheme would consist of damming a small valley high up on a mountain, and another one lower down, and then pumping water uphill with electrical power during glut periods and letting it run downhill again to drive turbines in periods of shortage. The pipes connecting the two lakes would be underground and invisible. The lakes themselves would be stocked with fish and would no doubt form homes for water birds and other aquatic kinds of life. But what was most remarkable about this conversation to me was that we were both sitting in front of a three bar electric fire:

'What do you suppose powers that?' I asked.

'Ah – but that's – different,' she replied.

Tidal barrages come in for the same opposition. The argument is generally that they will disturb the oyster catchers. The oyster catchers will be far more disturbed if the sea-level rises fifty feet as it is now prognosticated that it could do.

Perhaps the only thing that can save the world is that the fossil fuel is running out. But I don't think there is time for this to save us. We have got to stop burning fossil fuel because we want to – because we see the sense of it. We are, or suppose ourselves to be, rational beings; let us act rationally.

# TRANSPORT

# 3. Roads

Unless we come from a race of travelling people, we are all pretty much *locals*; we live somewhere, and what goes on in the locality in which we live is far more important to us than decisions made in some far-off 'capital' such as Paris, London, or Washington D.C. If we could once again run our lives on a local scale, with decisions taken on a local basis, then a lot of the most harmful trends in development on this planet would be stopped in their tracks.

If you look at the maps of most countries, or see them from an aeroplane, you will notice that there are two sorts of trackways or roads: there are the ancient roads that were made by local people to suit their interests; and cutting straight across the intricate organic pattern of the local roads you will generally find another pattern – the modern equivalent of the Roman roads. The railways, the trunk roads, and the motorways are the example *par excellence* of routes which contemptuously ignore all local features – they deviate neither to avoid, nor to take in, villages or towns – they just stride on oblivious of them. They ignore natural features, they cut through hills and stride over valleys on viaducts. These routes have been built by a metropolitan culture to serve its interests, and they were never seriously intended to serve the interests of the inhabitants of the countryside, or of the small towns and villages, in between the huge cities which they connect. The country inhabitants were not even consulted, or if they were their demands were not heeded.

This phenomenon of the latterday Roman roads illustrates very vividly the centralized, non-organic approach to the organization of society. We have come to believe that there is not Big Brother but Big Nanny up there, far away and never to be seen, and Nanny Knows Best. Nanny will tell us what to do and if we know what is good for us we'll do it.

The concept of the Nanny State has nothing to do with the gender of presidents or prime ministers, or indeed crowned heads of state. It has to do with the tendency of people who govern to believe that *they know best*. Therefore if the rest of us just do as they say, and don't argue, all will be well. And the larger countries are, the more powerful and *remote* Nanny is, and if we want a healthful and pleasant countryside again, and good small towns and villages, we should let Nanny quietly wither away. I submit we do not need her any more; we should each start playing our part in our local destiny. Government should grow from the ground up – not be imposed from the sky down. We should cease waiting for *them* to make decisions – we should make the decisions ourselves.

Most of the troubles of mankind are due to the fact that our communities, and our institutions, have got too big for us to handle or to understand. Our so-called democracies are far too big to be really democratic. In the Greek city state of the Golden Age of Greece every single citizen could make his voice heard. Does it really matter in the slightest whom you – or indeed I – vote for in the next general election? Well, my case may be different from yours because I have the luck to live in a nation of a civilized size. In travelling, and very often working, in at least forty

countries I have discovered that, without a single exception, life goes better for the inhabitants of small countries
than for big ones. I realize that in Periclean Athens there
were slaves who had no vote. This was bad, but it does
not invalidate what I say about the optimum size of
countries.

But to go back to the Roman roads. When William
Cobbett was riding on his horse throughout the English
shires he came upon a canal that was being dug, leading
from the West Country to London. Instead of writing in
his diary what a marvellous thing this was, because it
would encourage *trade*, he inveighed against it in good
old Cobbettian style, saying that it was just another
artery for draining the lifeblood out of the countryside to
swell what he called the *Wen*, the great cancerous sore
that was London as he saw it. While the country people,
who grew the wheat, were enfeebled by hunger, the corn
merchants were paying high prices to the farmers for
their crops and shipping them off to the big cities. The
only thing left for most of the poor country people to do
was to follow them, to go and join what Cobbett called
the ranks of the 'tax eaters'. The same canal that took the
good corn to London brought manufactured rubbish
back to sell to the remaining country people, got them
into debt to pay for it, and turned them into debt slaves.

There is no doubt that London, whether it could be
called a *Wen* or not, owed its extraordinary growth to the
canals and the great Thames that brought produce into it,
and, incidentally, carried the thousands of tons of *waste*
(most of it horse dung) away. The great fleet of East
Coast sailing barges contributed enormously to this. And
there is no doubt that it was the Roman roads that
enabled the city of Rome to grow to the swollen dimen-

sions that it achieved. The saying 'all roads lead to Rome' was true in more ways than one.

It is the proliferation of 'Romes' of today, all round the planet, which is, more than any other factor, destroying our world. There was a time when the size of a city was fixed by the number of miles that a horse-drawn wagon could travel in a day. A glance, for example, at the map of England, will show that market towns tend to be roughly thirty miles apart from each other. This distance was fixed by the ability of horse-drawn transport; farmers going to market, or wagoners carrying produce, could get from a place equidistant between two towns to one or other of them and home again the same day; cattle or sheep could be walked into the town in a day from the surrounding countryside. The population of the town was fixed by the same factors; it could not get too big because a population above a certain size could not be fed by the surrounding countryside.

Seaports could break out of this constraint, and they did so. Then came the canals, then the railways, and now the motorways, and this constraint of the *area of food supply* no longer applies anywhere. In every country the rural population crowds into the cities straining their resources, and the few people left in the countryside have to labour, desperately short-handed, to feed all those millions, and are thus forced to methods of husbandry that they do not really approve of. This is good neither for town nor country.

I would like to compare two villages I know. They might be anywhere, but in fact these particular ones are in Crete. One, high in the mountains, to the south of the mountain-cave where Zeus was born, can only be reached by an unpaved road full of ruts and potholes and quite unsuitable for buses. The only contact with the outside world that I could see was that a man with a tough little truck, with a load of fresh fish from the small fishing-port down on the coast, would brave the potholes and the ruts once a week and sell his fish. There must have been some export to gain the exchange for this import, and it was probably sheep. Two or three shepherds took their flocks high into the mountains to graze them there, and some of the increase of these flocks was no doubt driven down to the outer world to sell for money.

Otherwise the community was completely self-supporting. There were enough tiny terraced fields, with soil collected in them, to grow enough wheat for the people, although no surplus to sell. There were plenty of small vineyards and wine was so plentiful that it was virtually free. One man distilled spirits and *raki* was also so cheap that no price could realistically be set on it. Yet, surprisingly, there did not seem to be any drunks about the place. There was an oil mill for processing the large annual crop of olives. There were plenty of nut trees, orange and lemon groves, fig trees, and many other kinds of fruits. There were beehives and honey was plentiful. The sheep provided not only meat, in great abundance, but milk also, and there was splendid yoghurt and cheese. The people, as far as I could see, did not so much eat meals as *feast*. Every day was a feast day.

The houses were beautiful, simple, and extremely comfortable in that climate. Clothes were made by the women of the village. There was a loom-maker in a village not far away, a boot-maker in another village, a knife-maker in another. Spinning was done on the hand spindle and women spun wherever they went, for with a spindle you can spin and walk about at the same time. Nor was the weaving that they did purely utilitarian, it was extremely beautiful and decorative. Every girl, when she got married, inherited not only a loom, but a drawerful of beautiful cotton and wool garments and cloth that her mother had made in the years of her childhood. There was an ancient church in the village, and a youngish Greek Orthodox priest doubled as priest and school teacher. But the real education of the children, I believe, was carried on by the village as a whole: the children helped the grown ups in all their tasks and business, they wandered freely into any house, and the adults passed on to them the lore and legends of the community.

The villagers paid no taxes to any central government. They knew their own laws and kept them because they were theirs. There was, indeed, a 'policeman' who lived in the village. He and the mayor and I were once walking down the steep street, going from one house of hospitality to another because – as always – feasting was going on, and the mayor put his hand down his shirt and pulled out a revolver. He fired several shots into the air: a *feu de joie*. He then laughed loudly, brandished the pistol, and said to me 'This man ought to arrest me. I have no gun licence!' Every man in that village had a firearm, and yet there was no crime. They all had a fear that the Turks, who had ruled Crete for centuries very brutally, might one day try to come back.

Was there culture, you might well ask? Well there was singing, music and dancing in plenty, and no doubt much telling of old stories and epics. I have no doubt that Homer lived in just such a village. There were few books, although everybody could read. If they had wanted books they could have obtained them, but the village always hummed with lively conversation.

The other Cretan village I wish to describe was lower down in the mountains and had just had a 'good' road driven to it. The road was the worst thing that could ever have happened to it and would end up by destroying it. Firstly it had brought a rich man up from the city who started offering the peasants what were to them large sums of money for their land. They sold it to him. He started a process of stumping out all the ancient olive trees to replant with new, quick-growing dwarf olive trees, from which the olives would be easy to pick for sale. The result was that the villagers were already having to spend money on olive oil; they were being dragged headlong into a money economy. Then all sorts of traders began to come up into the village; a small supermarket opened up. The villagers were beginning to find that they 'needed' all sorts of articles that they had never needed before. So they had to grow more crops than they really needed, so that they could sell the surplus to buy the rubbish in the supermarket. Instead of eating such food as walnuts dipped in honey – which was commonplace in the village higher up – they were now buying foreign packet 'instant' desserts from the supermarket and thinking they were onto something wonderful. Instead of drinking their own good wine – or the juice from their own orange and lemon trees – they were buying fizzy flavoured sugar-water from the shop. No doubt they were ruining their teeth with it. Television was creeping in, and making the people of that village dissatisfied with their lot. Having seen how the imaginary inhabitants of Dallas lived – they too wanted to live somewhere like Dallas. The young people were no longer singing and dancing in the old way. That seemed to them now provincial and *passé*. They wanted American culture – American songs, dances and music.

To many of the youngsters of both sexes the new road *looked* like a road to freedom – but would prove to be, alas, a road to sadness and discontent. And once they had gone down it they would never come back again. The old, stable economy of their village was gone for ever, there would be no place for them there. A few chosen people would find paid employment there, working for the new wealthy class that was taking over everything; the old people would eventually die and no doubt the young would find their way across the Atlantic.

I fully realize that in painting the picture of these two Cretan villages I will be opening myself to the charge of 'Nannyism' myself. Who am I to know what Cretan peasants want, or don't want. Who am I to know what is good for other people – I hardly know what is good for myself! And yet I have a right to give other people my advice, and if I were to advise the inhabitants of the first village I described I would say to them: do not allow your village to be taken over by outside business interests, do not voluntarily throw away your ancient independence and self sufficiency, and do not leave your beautiful home to go in search of the 'Dallas' of your imaginings because it does not really exist. And, after all, they don't have to listen to what I say or take any notice of me, do they?

The motorways of Europe push out from the industrial heartland like the arms of a great devouring octopus, and suck the real wealth out of the land, take industrial rubbish back in exchange, and bring noise, discontent and pollution wherever they go. They flatten out everything, destroy local tradition and local culture, and make us all the same. Fortunately the oil will have run out before this vast devil's network is completed. I have a little plan ready for when that happens: people with jackhammers will use the last few dregs of the world's oil, drilling little 'pop holes' – as miners call them – every four feet all along the motorways. Quarter sticks of gelignite will be put down these holes and detonated, and trees will be planted in the little craters thus made. Linear forests will snake about our world instead of the linear rat-race tracks that are polluting it now.

And meanwhile, we that have to live before this happens, let us ignore the present day 'Roman roads' as much as we can, and concentrate on the organic network of human trackways that was there before them, and will be there after they have gone. Let us labour to make beautiful our own beloved localities, where we actually have to live. Let us pay as little tribute as we possibly can to Nanny and her myriad servants. Let us devote our wealth and treasure to improving our own localities. Let us labour to achieve the sort of local self-sufficiency that will give us *real* prosperity, not just 'bytes' of financial information on computer somewhere. Let us live so that we may all eat walnuts dipped in honey, and drink our own good wine, or beer, or cider, and revive our old cultural traditions again, that have been damaged nearly to death by the mega-culture brought by the Roman roads.

The ozone layer will not be saved by Nanny and her edicts, nor will these edicts save our world from acid rain or the greenhouse effect. There is not time, we cannot wait for Nanny, we must do it ourselves. We on the nursery floor must take our destiny into our own hands; we must start building, now, a new civilization to take the place of the one that has proved unworthy and is destroying our world. The City of God will not be built from above down; it will be built by us, by the hands of men and women, and it will be built from the ground up.

# 4. Cars

Now we tackle one of the thorniest and most difficult subjects of all: the motor car. Of all the conveniences of modern times this is the hardest to imagine giving up. Trains never seem to go where we want to go, or when. A long distance coach is an ordeal-on-wheels, at least it is for this traveller. We motorists have got into the habit of starting a journey when we like, breaking it wherever and whenever we like, travelling as far or as slowly as we like and ending up exactly where we want. You don't even have to *pack* to go on a journey with a car: you simply 'fling everything into the car' and off you go.

The motorist has come to be the modern equivalent of the *hidalgo* – the cavalier. In days of old the man who did not ride a horse was felt to be, and probably felt himself to be, inferior. It was the noble knights who charged the enemy on horses, *hoi-polloi* were the footmen: The horse is dead – long live the motor car!

Men – including men old enough to be more sensible – look upon their car as a statement of their masculinity. If you do not believe that just look at car advertisements or go to the motor show. Even countries which have imposed strict speed limits are not allowed, by their predominantly masculine car lobby, to limit the potential speed of cars – the one measure that would really cut down accidents. This is because the speed that my car *could* go at, if I were allowed to drive it thus, is a measure of my virility.

Little tiny boys prefer above everything to play with little tiny toy motor cars. (When I was a little tiny boy some of us still ran about astride hobby horses.) If we don't prevent them, when they get less tiny, they pinch real motor cars and smash them up and get into trouble with the police. Some of us, hopefully, grow up. Some of us manage to sublimate this desire to augment our puny bodies with fast and noisy machines. Some of us turn to mountain climbing, or sailing in small boats, or rowing them, or horse riding, or long-distance running or activities which actually improve and test the power of our brains and bodies; there is nobody outside an institution who cannot be taught to drive a motor car. You do not demonstrate your intelligence, or the power of your muscles, by sitting on a cushion pressing a pedal with your right foot and gently moving a steering wheel with your hand. You did not design the machine, nor make it (quite possibly you couldn't even change the sparking plugs), you did not drill for the oil, nor refine it, and you prove nothing about your sexual potency by screaming along a motorway at a hundred and twenty miles an hour. You merely prove that you are a fool.

Many women claim that they could not do without a motor car because of its extreme convenience to them. I can certainly understand this. Many women have to do a lot of shopping. Housewives, contrary to what we are told ought to be the case, really do exist. They often have to operate accompanied by children. There is nothing in the world more convenient than being able to strap the kids in the kiddy-seats in the back and drive straight up to a shop and load your purchases in there and then. And then drive right up to your front door with them. Better than slogging about in the rain with a baby on your back in a baby-sling, two older ones hanging on to your skirts and screaming their heads off because you didn't let 'em get at the chocs by the cash till, with your hands full of heavy plastic carrier bags, and then having to wait endlessly for a bus before you learn that there is a go-slow at the bus depot. Would it really be reasonable for someone like me to advise a woman in that predicament to forego her motor car?

I have a friend who lives in a castle in Ireland and who became so worried about the morals of owning a motor car that he drove his into a field, filled it up with straw, and set light to it. The police came and took his shotgun away because they thought he had gone mad and he now drives his wife's car instead.

But what are the arguments against driving a motor car? Well, the arguments that we all can see are: cars are noisy, cars are dangerous, cars are smelly and cause ill-health, cars make us lazy which also causes ill-health, cars destroy the peace of the countryside and the amenity of the towns. But the great argument, which is not so readily apparent, is that cars, in excess, are destroying our planet and rendering it unfit for animal life. For, even if the jungle-burners stay their hand, the emissions from car exhausts will go on destroying the forests and releasing more and more carbon dioxide into the atmosphere. They will go on destroying the ozone layer which is our only defence against skin cancer and, far more important, protects the growth of green plants. The production of cars is enormously polluting, and so is the construction of the roads to carry them.

But when it comes to stopping driving our cars excessively we come up against the Tragedy of the Commons again. If everyone in the world could be stopped from driving private motor cars the world would be a much happier, cleaner, quieter and more salubrious place. But if I alone stopped driving my motor car it would make no appreciable difference at all. Therefore why should I? And we all think like this and go on driving our motor cars.

In 1978 the Oak Ridge National Laboratory, researching for the United States government, said that in that year there were 300 million motor vehicles in the world but by the year 2000 there would be 700 million. Now considering the damage that was already being done to the environment by the 300 million what sort of disaster would be caused if the figure really did rise to 700 million? And what would the figure be like in say 2020?

And yet we, who have motor cars, can scarcely deny them to the world's millions who have them not. What about the *Chinese* housewife with three screaming children and a clutch of shopping bags?

People with motor cars are not going to give them up until they are forced to. One day they will be, but meanwhile the only sensible advice to give them is: use them less. If you really wish to live as though the world mattered, if you are really concerned that posterity shall inherit a beautiful and un-poisoned planet – then *use your car far less*. There should be a tape-recording in every car which turns itself on when you start the engine and growls at you: 'Is your journey really necessary?' Nine times out of ten, if you were really honest about it, you would answer 'No.'

Do you really have to drive out of town to that supermarket, or hypermarket or whatever they like to call it? Can you go to the local shop round the corner? You may think you are paying a few pennies more in the latter but don't forget the money you save by not 'hopping in the car'. Also, if you use the local shop it will become more competitive and bring its prices down; you may even *save* the local shop. I spent some months in a suburb of San Francisco where there were no local shops left: you *had* to drive ten miles to a huge supermarket, which had a monopoly and was charging any prices it wanted to. The complete absence of small shops was an awful deprivation to the area – the quality of life was the worse for their absence – and their demise was made inevitable by the 'hop-in-the-car' attitude. Of course when you reach that stage of 'civilization', you *have* to have a car – you are completely dependent upon it – you would simply starve if you did not have one.

You do *not* have to hop in the car to 'nip round to the pub'. If you walk to the pub you will enjoy your beer far more when you get there, and if you walk home afterwards you will not be breathalysed, you will sleep the better for it and you will wake up next morning without a hangover. You will also have the satisfaction of knowing, as you swig your pints, that you are not harming the environment in any way.

There is a concept which I invented many years ago, but which the faculties of philosophy of the world's universities have so far failed to take up (not being able to recognize a good thing when they see it). It is the principle of P.D.O.A. This principle is illustrated perfectly by the person who gets in the car and drives five miles to a 'health centre', and there sits for half an hour pedalling a stationary exercise bicycle, and then drives home again.

The letters stand for Principle of Diametrically Opposing Aims. The person who buys a motorized lawn-mower to cut the grass of a pocket handkerchief-sized lawn – and next week goes and buys an 'exercise machine' to instal in the bathroom, is another great exponent of P.D.O.A. A beautiful example of the Principle in action is the gadget which turns butter into cream. People expend much energy turning cream into butter – and then here is this instrument for turning it back into cream again. A long book will be written one day by some learned person giving examples of P.D.O.A. from all over the world.

In 1987 the Oak Ridge National Laboratory in Tennessee published the following table. It shows the *calories of energy* used up, per passenger/kilometre, by various modes of travel.

| Travel Type | Calories/km |
|---|---|
| Automobile with one occupant | 1,153 |
| Bus | 570 |
| Rail | 549 |
| Walking | 62 |
| Bicycling | 22 |

Of course it must be remembered that the last two modes of transport, although they use energy, do not use fossil fuel energy. A cyclist, we are told, can cycle 5.6 kilometres on an ear of maize. The motorist uses 52½ times as much energy as the cyclist and thus pumps out 52½ times as much $CO_2$, besides a lot of other nasties that the cyclist does not produce. Also, the energy the cyclist uses is re-newable energy – energy collected by the corn plant from the sun by photosynthesis; the eating of that ear of corn does not make demands on the world's dwindling fossil fuel supplies.

I have been in cities, some in Holland and at least one in the United States (Davis, California) where the cyclist has been properly catered for, and have seen that whenever this has happened thousands of people cycle. A few hardy souls cycle in such places as London and New York but, what with the exhaust fumes and the danger to life and limb, they seem to me to be nothing less than heroic. But as such cities become more and more congested, and the authorities at last realize that, short of pulling the whole city down and building it again underground, there is no other cure for the traffic problem, more and more cities will adopt this option. Whole systems of streets will be closed to motor traffic, and opened to cyclists and pedestrians, who will thus be able to travel about their cities in peace and comfort and immeasurably improve their health at the same time.

Gradually, as our cities are freed of motor traffic, the air will get purer, the streets will get safer and more pleasant, and it will be a pleasure to walk or cycle again. This is the sensible radical alternative.

But radical treatment must be applied to other aspects of our cities as well. There was a time when huge cities such as London and Birmingham in England were collections of villages. Until the end of World War Two the industrial city of Birmingham was organized so that every small part of it had at least one factory to employ people, a complete set of shops to supply people, a school, a library, a public swimming pool and those mysteriously-named 'slipper baths', an assortment of pubs, and churches of various denominations. A person could live in such a district from the cradle to the grave and never go out of it if he or she didn't want to. Of course most people did go out of their areas, either to the city centre where there were facilities which the district could not supply, or to the country or seaside for a change of scene altogether.

Now, that particular city, Birmingham, has no such locally organized infrastructure: it has completely broken down. You live in a housing estate in one place and commute perhaps ten miles to your work in another place. The small shops have died and so you have to go to the centre for shopping; your children have to be bussed miles to some huge school, where they feel themselves to be strangers because the other kids are not from their area; and the old feeling of pride in one's locality and pleasure in being there has broken down. When you go to the pub you do not find your workmates there – for everybody else is commuting huge distances to their work too. You do not know your neighbours any more.

The answer to the problem of commuting to and from work in huge cities can only be solved by *having less commuting!* Find work near where you live. There is no industry there? Then start one! My old friend Professor Leopold Kohr, who has thought and spoken and written perhaps more than any other man on the subject, said to me once: 'Where I live, in Aberystwyth, I am within three hundred yards of: my work, my bank, my doctor, my lawyer, the sea, the country, a library, a university, six pubs, six churches, every kind of shop I could possibly want to go to, and a railway station. What do I need with a car?'

The industrial and commercial infrastructure of both town and country has adapted itself to an era of very cheap, and almost universal, motorized transport. The result of this has not made for a beautiful, healthful, sociable and convivial world at all. It has produced an ugly world and a polluting and unhealthy world. We must change it.

We will have to change it anyway when the oil gets scarcer. Let us change it now of our own volition before this happens! Let us work, individually and together, for a world of self-sufficient self-contained localities – parishes perhaps – where one individual can comprehend, and influence creatively, the whole; where you can walk to anywhere you really need to go; where you can find all the fun, culture and conviviality the human soul desires within range of your own two legs. Then, when you want some extra buzz, or to buy some rather special item, there can be good public transport to take you to the city centre, or another locality of the same city, or the country, or another city. There could be more taxis too. Plying along fairly traffic-free streets these would provide far quicker, more comfortable, and less polluting transport than they do now.

The attempt to solve the commuter problem by driving yet more tunnels through Mother Earth, building more multi-story car parks, pulling down yet more of the city to widen roads will never ever work. It will only cause more congestion, more confusion and more pollution. It will continue to fill the hospitals and drive people to drink. We must organize our world so that we need to do far *less* commuting, that is the only effective way of tackling the problem.

We are constantly told nowadays that the electronic revolution will render commuting to work less and less necessary: people will be able to stay at home and conduct all their business by telephone, telex, fax and all the rest of it. This does not seem to be happening, even in jobs in which it could happen. My limited experience of the office-working world suggests that people *want to be there* – they are dead scared of being lapped in the office rat-race. And, of course, in the jobs that women and men do actually to produce something tangible, like a loaf of bread, or a bag of coal, or a pair of trousers, it cannot happen. You *have* to go there, to the site where the production is actually taking place.

We are all aware that most of the cars screaming along our motorways are company cars. That new-looking vehicle that has just overtaken us in that perilous manner, driven by a man with a collar and tie on, is rushing up to some place like Nuneaton to show some samples of gentlemen's socks to a shop-keeper who could perfectly well get them through the post. There is no good reason for this army of men tearing backwards and forwards up and down the countryside with little cases full of samples.

The firms that employ them should be made to pay for the pollution they cause! This great army of frenetic salespeople is doing more damage to the atmosphere and the ozone layer than perhaps many other factors put together! They should be stopped in their tracks; their journeys are not really necessary at all. They should be given creative work to do. God knows enough such work needs to be done in our suffering old planet.

As for that other great polluting army, the drivers of heavy goods vehicles, they should gradually be demobilized too. We – you and I – can secure their demobilization: simply insist always on buying locally-produced goods, whenever you can, wherever you can; boycott the stuff brought from far away; support your neighbours. If there could be a widespread concerted movement, nationwide or worldwide, to do just this, work – good work – could be found for all those redundant lorry drivers. And anyway the cab of an HGV is not a healthy or pleasant place in which to spend your working life.

The most urgent task for all we who believe our planet really matters is to transform a world that has been adapted, hurriedly and badly, to suit the needs of the motor vehicle, into a world fit for human beings to live in again: fit for men, women and children.

As I have said, I was born in 1914 and if I live to be a hundred I believe I shall have lived right through the automobile age, from practically its start to practically its finish. In terms of human history it will have been as the blinking of an eye. And in spite of the enormous convenience of petrol-driven vehicles, I believe that life will be incomparably richer without them.

# WORK AND HOME

# 5. Work

I once knew an old lady who lived by herself in the Golden Valley of Herefordshire. She was one of the happiest old women I have ever met. She described to me all the work that she and her mother used to do when she was a child: washing on Monday, butter-making on Tuesday, market on Wednesday and so on. 'It all sounds a lot of hard work!' I said to her.

'Yes but nobody had ever told us then,' she said, in her soft Herefordshire accent.

'Told you what?'

'Told us there was anything *wrong* with work!'

*Work* has become a dirty word and it connotes an evil thing. Nowadays most people would do anything to get out of work. To say that an invention is 'labour-saving' is to give it the ultimate accolade. The fact that the labour it saves might be good labour, and enjoyable, is never considered possible. Able-bodied people even invent methods (albeit never very effective ones) of *gardening* without *digging* – because they are so shy of work. If they dug they would have better gardens and stronger backs.

Since the Industrial Revolution most work has become repetitive, degrading, and above all *boring*. I have ploughed all day behind a pair of good horses and been sad when the day came to an end and I had to unhitch them (the horses might have felt differently, but they always seemed keen enough to go out to the field in the morning).

But for most workers in big factories or in modern offices the working day has become an ordeal of grinding *boredom*. They are left so drained of life and joy at the end of it that all they have the heart for is to slump in front of a television set with a six-pack of lager.

This book is about changing our lifestyles, and I am aware that no subject is as important as this one, nor as fraught with difficulties. The young couple who have mortgaged themselves up to the eyebrows to buy a house, have to pay a huge sum monthly for their season tickets to get to work and back, have a bank overdraft and a debit with the credit-card sharks, are in no position to be choosy over what *work* they do.

Why *should* we get into such a situation? Why *should* we all labour to enrich the banks, for that is what we are doing? Why *should* so many of us have to travel hours a day in crowded and uncomfortable transport to and from our workplaces? If the inhabitant of the Western world considers her or his situation she or he will probably come to the conclusion that *usury* is at the bottom of most of the problems of life. It is the constraint of usury that forces people to work at jobs that bore them and from which they obtain no satisfaction whatever. Until the six-teenth century in Europe lending money at interest was simply not allowed. Christianity would not countenance it; the Islamic religion will not countenance it; Judaism would not countenance it as a transaction between Jews, but lending money to non-Jews was allowed. This is why, in Europe, Jews became the first money lenders; they were allowed to do what Christians were not allowed to do.

With the Reformation, and the virtual collapse of Christianity, usury flourished. The whole world began to get into debt. The population began to divide itself into two classes: creditors and debtors. Our capitalist economy is founded on debt. The most radical and beneficial change any person could make to his or her lifestyle is to get out of debt. I know, from my own experience, this is easier said than done. But it can be done.

Our capitalist society creates never-ending *wants*. It causes industry to conduct endless research to produce ever more numerous substances and articles, and to keep bringing out more *lines*. Most of the lines that were invented in Victorian times, and considered so essential then, have long since been abandoned as people found out that they were not essential at all. The same fate, please God, will befall most of the new lines we consider so essential today.

After all – what does a man or a woman really want? Good food, good shelter, clothing, adequate transport, adequate warmth, access to culture, love. There is nothing else. Once those seven needs have been supplied surely we should be free to enjoy our brief lives on this planet? And should those simple needs be too difficult to provide for?

There are two kinds of work: good work and bad work. The first is the finest thing we are ever likely to discover during our lifetimes. The second is probably the worst. Good work gives significance to our lives, bad work causes a sickness of the spirit. Forced to choose between these two kinds of work – no matter how much the second kind may be loaded with high profit or high wages – we should unhesitatingly choose the first. To toil at a boring and pointless task all one's working life in order to pile up money in the bank is surely the most pointless exercise any human being can engage in. He or she, while alive, will not have the spirit or leisure to enjoy the fruits of that wealth and will not be able to take any of it with them when they die: not a farthing. That life will have been entirely wasted.

I remember once, I was working aboard the sailing-barge 'Cambria' – skipper and owner my old friend Bob Roberts. She was smashing through the choppy sea with a fresh beam wind and 175 tons of wheat in her belly. Bob and I stood one each side of the great teak wheel because the weight of wind was such that she was carrying a lot of helm and one man could not steer her, with the great towering spread of red canvas, cordage and spars slanted away to leeward overhead. Bob saw the joy and excitement in my eyes and said: 'You know John – people sweat out their lives doing boring work in city offices just to make enough money to do this for a fortnight every year. *I* do it all the time – *and get paid for it*!' That was *good* work – and sad it is that very few of us get to do it now.

And I think that bad work depresses our spirits and bores us nigh to death as much as anything because we know in our hearts that it is damaging our planet, which it almost always is. Our world has gone wrong because we have taken one factor and one factor only into consideration, and that is money. Other factors, such as happiness, health, social justice, the rights of our posterity, or the need to care for our planet, have never been considered by economists, industrialists, or governments. If something *makes money* it must be good; economists have never been asked to apply their Law of Diminishing Returns, for example, to anything else except *money*. To increase the size of an industry may be to increase the profits the industrialist is getting on his capital – up to a point at which diminishing returns set in. Then, maybe because size becomes excessive, the profit on increasing the size further begins to level off – then to fall away.

But supposing you applied the same Law of Diminishing

Returns to other things *besides* money? The health, happiness and well-being of the workers perhaps? You might find that diminishing returns in those things set in far sooner than they do when the consideration is just money. Or suppose you considered the welfare of our planet? To make the company bigger and bigger until it swallows up all the other companies in the same industry may make a bigger *profit* – but it is almost certain to be more damaging to our planet. Money is a very good invention and is very useful but we should not make it the *only* gauge of our enterprises. When we do so, all other considerations become forgotten, and we end up by destroying our happiness, damaging our health, putting intolerable strain on our families and hurting our planet.

I am not claiming that profit-making in itself destroys or damages our planet. Everyone who creates anything that humankind requires must make a profit or cease to operate. There is nothing wrong – everything right – with making a profit. But when the profit-making activity damages the world we have to live in then of course it is wrong. When this happens we should find some other way of making a profit.

I have met hundreds of people, in many countries and four continents, who have withdrawn themselves from the big-industry rat-race and, moving to the country or else staying in town or city, have found good, honest and honourable ways to make a living producing useful and beautiful goods or providing services. Some are fairly well-off with regard to *money*: others are poor in that respect, but they are rich in the things that really matter. They are the people of the future. If they are not in debt they are happy men and women.

There is only one thing that is considered worse than

*work* in our industrial countries and that is *no work*. No fate is considered more horrible than that; whenever anyone complains that this or that industry is polluting, or unpleasant, or degrading to the people who have to work in it, the answer is: 'Oh – so you want to throw people on the dole do you?'

But almost invariably you will find, if you look into it, that it is those very polluting industries I have described which do throw people on the dole in the first place. The agro-chemical industry provides employment and therefore must be preserved at any cost? Well in fact the employment it provides is minimal: in terms of jobs per thousand pounds of investment its record is abysmal. And the unemployment it creates is enormous! Chemicals replace labour on the farm, that is their chief function; you poison weeds so you don't have to pay somebody to hoe them.

To close down a nuclear power station because it is dangerous and polluting will 'put people out of work'? Well if you replaced that nuclear power station with a new small industry, or a group of small industries, to improve house insulation so that not so much electrical power would be needed; or if you started small factories to make wind or water or solar electricity generators, you would not only employ every person displaced from the nuclear power station, but you would be looking round for more people. Schumacher was the first economist as far as I know to study seriously the problem of how many jobs are created by a given capital investment. He found that the *bigger* an industry was, and the more 'high-tech', the more capital it needed to establish one workplace. You can set someone up as a village carpenter with a couple of thousand pounds: it takes millions to give someone a job in the nuclear power industry. If we want to solve unemployment we want investment in labour-intensive industries: not capital-intensive ones. We want more small industries: fewer huge ones. We want more true crafts-people – more apprentices to them.

We should liberalize the planning laws, which at present are the chief constraints against such developments. It should be a basic right of all citizens to establish their own workshop on their own land. In Wales an official of CoSIRA, the ridiculously named body set up by the government to encourage small industry in the country-side, told me that he was completely disillusioned by his job. Whenever he had laboured to help some person to set up a small workshop somewhere his plans were thwarted by the planning authorities – which turned down any application either to build a new workshop or convert existing redundant farm buildings. Our young people are forced to leave the countryside and go and join the dole queues in London and other cities. Yet if an oil company wants to set up a huge refinery in a national park it usually ends up getting planning permission; the company merely has to say 'It will create jobs.' But the jobs it will create are negligible in number, since it takes very few people to run an oil refinery. The same amount of *capital* put into creating a large number of small industries and workshops would create far more jobs, and honest jobs too.

We would be wise to plan *now* for drastic changes that could be forced on us. If I were a 'high flyer' in a merchant bank, or a finance company, I would start learning an honest trade now. A person in such a position must feel utterly secure: it must seem to them that, so long as the ulcers spare them, their world will last for ever and ever. Well I submit it won't.

When I search my mind to think of people who have managed, in one way or another, to get out of the rat-race, I find myself utterly amazed by the number of such people that I know, and the enormous diversity of the solutions they have found for themselves. It is a cliché now to talk of people who live in some idyllic cottage in the country and programme computers. Yes, I have known several such people, and they seem to be doing all right. I do not share the current gung-ho attitude to computers – I am sure they will be found to have some peripheral uses one day but show me a computer that can grow a sack of potatoes and I'll take them much more seriously. But meanwhile, while the computer euphoria lasts, it seems a good way to live in a beautiful place and make a living.

After all, what does it take to make an honest living? If one is not in debt, and has a house, and a workshop if need be, and happily a big garden, or an allotment, in which to grow some fresh vegetables, it is surprising what a good life one can have on very little money.

I am very much aware of the problems that arise when city people remove to the country, and set up their homes and their means of making a living there. Firstly, they push up the price of houses so that the locals, dependent on rural incomes and economics, cannot buy them, and so there is a complementary drift to the cities: it becomes simply an exchange of populations with city people moving to the country and country people, driven out by high house prices, moving the other way. But this phenomenon is caused by one thing only: repressive and out-dated planning laws. We have *got* to let people buy land at fair prices (i.e. the agricultural value or a little more) and build houses on it. This is a problem that simply need not be.

I know a village in north Devon, very remote, far from

any railway, in which reside and earn their livings: a blacksmith, specializing in original ornamental work, two potters, both highly professional people who make good livings at serious enterprises; a full-time professional typesetter, a local newspaper, a publisher (Green Books) which has now published some two dozen titles; a magazine publisher (*Resurgence*); a chair-maker (or two actually because husand and wife both work in the small but highly mechanized workshop in the back garden). Most of these people, with the exception of Mr Honeybear the blacksmith, are drop-ins from far away. They have come there because it is a beautiful place. But they integrate well with the indigenous society. The chair-maker husband is a member of the fire brigade and has to carry a bleeper; one of the potters runs the boy scouts. All these people make a good living and they lack for nothing that an honest man or woman should want. They all have good and comfortable homes. They all, for better or for worse, own motor cars. They are as secure as one can be in an uncertain world.

This village is unusual in that, besides a very good primary school, it has a privately-run 'alternative' sec-ondary school, which currently has thirty children in it. This was set up to avoid local children having to be 'bussed' thirty miles away to the nearest juvenile sausage-factory (I cannot call such places *schools*). The village has, of course, all the traditional and usual commercial enterprises, such as three pubs, a cafe, a fish and chip shop, a video library, several jobbing builders, an undertaker, and the owner of a small fleet of buses. There are two good car mechanics. There is a baker who bakes *real bread*.

Near the village is an old watermill. The most noble thing anybody could do is to buy it up and turn it into a working mill again, grind grist for the local farmers and bread flour –

from organically grown wheat and rye preferably – for the local bakers and housewives.

I have detailed the various craft activities of this village to indicate that, if people tackle it seriously and professionally and really prepare themselves for a new life, they *can* go somewhere pleasant and make a living which is not damaging to the world. We do *not* all have to work for huge organizations. And as more and more such people move to places like Hartland, and establish a living there, the general economy of the place is stimulated and the local people, who have always lived there, benefit too. Instead of the village shops having to close their doors they can keep going. More and more people find they can earn a good living.

You may well say that a proliferation of studio potters, country chair-makers, and all the rest of it is not going to be sufficient to sustain the economy of a modern industrial country. Well, indeed, there must be bigger factories too. Some no doubt in cities and towns, some in the country. In the little market town near to me here in Ireland a man and his two sons run a blast furnace in a small town garden! When it is fired, as it is once a week, it looks like a volcano in full eruption. They cast manhole covers for the county council, and anything else anybody wants. Their stock is scrap iron, or steel, that is brought to them mostly by Travelling people, and thus they serve a marvellous function turning rubbish into useful articles.

I do not want to see the dismantling of all big industry. I want to see the dismantling of polluting or damaging big industry. I want to see the production of artefacts which will last. One of the few things I require from big factories is a typewriter. I suppose I carried half a dozen modern typewriters to the dump before a son-in-law made me a present of the one I am using now. It is dated 1940, so has given various people fifty years of service, and shows every sign of giving at least fifty more – although it won't be me who is banging it. No doubt the English factory that produced it was forced to close down by factories producing the cheap, ephemeral plastic rubbish that floods the markets now and which I was continually carting off to the landfill site. The production of most manufactured articles may have to be, to some extent, polluting, to some extent destructive of non-renewable resources. Isn't it incumbent on us to insist that such articles be made to *last* for as long as possible? *Nearly* all the articles we require for the good life can be produced in the workshops of good professional craftspeople. The few things that cannot are best made in small factories (as small as is consistent with doing the job) staffed by competent and professional people, such as the people who made this typewriter.

I believe Gordon Bottomley said it all in his poem 'To Iron-founders and Others':

> When the old hollowed earth is cracked,
>     And when, to grasp more power and feasts,
> Its ores are emptied, wasted, lacked,
>     The middens of your burning beasts
>
> Shall be raked over till they yield
>     Last priceless slags for fashionings high,
> Ploughs to wake grass in every field,
>     Chisels men's hands to magnify.

## Postscript

The first time I visited Inishmor, the biggest of the three Aran Islands that lie in the mouth of Galway Bay, I was in the company of an American, or at least an Aran islander who had emigrated to America half a lifetime before. We were greeted on landing by his brother, who had never left the island in his life. The American brother looked puffy and unhealthy, he had suffered, he told me, from gastric ulcers and his heart wasn't too good. The islander brother looked as fit and hard as it was possible for a man to be. He got his living by a mixture of smallholding and fishing, and the fishing was done in the curach, which had to be rowed, and you had to be fit to do that work.

The American brother was rich. He wanted to establish an aeroplane landing strip on the island, and a restaurant, and a tourist trade, and God knows what else. The islander brother wasn't too keen on all this.

'Have you got any unemployment on this island?' asked the American. The islander thought for some time before answering this. He found the question quite difficult. Then he said: 'There is nobody *employed* here – we have no *employment*.'

'Do you mean none of you do any *work*?'

Of course, anyone can see, you couldn't live on that island, unless you worked long and hard. 'Well we *work*,' said the islander. 'But no one here is employed.'

I loved that attitude to work. But the American brother could not understand it, and, inevitably, the airstrip came, and the restaurants, and the tourists, and all the rest of it. The islanders are certainly not any happier – they have far more to worry them. And the island is certainly far less magical and beautiful. If only they could have left it alone.

# 6. Home

Here is a quotation from *The Simple Home* written by an American, Charles Keeler, in 1904:

> Home making is one of the sacred tasks of life, for the home is the family temple . . . The building of the home should be an event of profound importance. It should be with men as it is with birds, the culminating event after courtship and marriage, upon which all the loving thought and energy of the bridal pair is bestowed.

Keeler goes on to describe the generation of the sort of 'home' that most Americans apparently did live in in his day:

> The real estate agent and the investor confer, and as a result we have rows of houses put up to sell, to shiftless house seekers who are too indifferent to think about their needs, and helplessly take what has been built for the trade. The taint of commercialism is over these homes, and all too often the life within them is shallow and artificial.

In the effort to change our lifestyles for the better the quality of the *home* we live in is more important than anything else. If we live in boring and unsatisfying dwellings ('all made out of ticky-tacky' as the song has it) we will not be contented, no matter how much money we have. We will be constantly trying to divert ourselves with this or that new gadget, electronic or otherwise; we will always be giving way to the urge to 'jump in the car', or 'hop on a 'plane' – to rush off somewhere hoping to find that which we cannot find at home. Such anodynes do not make us happy. They can never be more than substitutes for the real thing we lack: a good, beautiful and loving home. A home in which we can revive the lost art of hospitality, a home where true culture, real conviviality, real fun, solid comfort and, above all, real civilization, can be had.

My belief is that much of the restlessness of contemporary humankind – the endless searching for we know not what which is so corrosive to our planet – stems from the fact that we do not have satisfying homes. And homes cannot be made in factories, nor by computers or machines: they must be – like communion wine – 'the work of human hands'. The most creative thing that anybody can do in this world is to make a home. I have heard a woman say: 'I am only a housewife!' *Only* a housewife! If she had said: 'I am only Prime Minister,' I would have commiserated with her. As it was she had the most creative and certainly the most important job on Earth.

No doubt the home-maker is more important than the house. I have seen real homes created in the most boring of council houses, or even in shacks. Just after the Second World War I spent several days as a guest in one of the 'native' shanty towns that had grown up, illegally, to the west of Johannesburg in South Africa. The 'house' I stayed in had been built out of flattened petrol cans. The narrow alleys to the front and the back of it were filthy, the sanitary arrangements were appalling, the building was bloody cold at night and roasting hot in the day; but it was a *real home*. The walls inside were hung all over with bright coloured cloths, and with pictures, mostly cut out of magazines, the furniture, knocked up from old packing cases, was adequate, lively children ran in and out, and if there were not enough chairs for them there were always enough adult laps, people were constantly dropping in, and talking and laughing, and singing, and playing tunes on a mouth organ, and arguing, and smiling. You do not need a mansion to create a home.

I was privileged as a little boy, not because I lived in a manor house (which I did) but because I used to be *dumped*, from time to time, in the cottage that had been the home of Annie Fisher, who was by way of being my nanny. Annie's dad was head horseman on a farm at Landermere, in Essex. Like all head horsemen he was proud and pretty dignified. He had a large moustache and smelled of horses and shag tobacco. But he loved children, his eyes smiled even if the rest of his face did not, and once on a Sunday he took me down to the tidal water at Landermere to show me how to fish for crabs with a piece of meat tied to a string.

There were five children still at home and not really enough room for us all but nobody minded that. There were only two bedrooms upstairs. Downstairs was a Front Room, which was kept as a sacred place in case any of the gentry called, or for occasional polite tea parties; it was like a sort of shrine to gentility and seemed to me to be a great waste of space, although children could sit and read in it, with a comic or a book, provided they kept quiet and didn't break any of the useless little knick-knacks that cluttered every horizontal surface. The kitchen, however, was a fair-sized room and was, without any doubt whatever, the heart of the home. Next door was a cool larder.

Outside the back door was a small brick building known as the Backus, Essex for 'back house'. It contained two big coppers, one for doing the laundry and the other for boiling up a cow's head, or a ham, or for making wine or any other such uses. The walls of the kitchen were decorated with prints depicting such scenes as 'The Soldier's Farewell' or 'Young Love'. There was a fine dresser with willow-pattern plates and dishes on it, several solid well-polished country chairs – rendered almost black with time – a massive deal table scrubbed as white as snow, a couple of corner cupboards and – the heart of the heart – the beautiful cast-iron coal-burning range, kept lovingly black-leaded by Mrs Fisher. The fire door of the range was generally open and the coals burned red behind the bars. A sailing barge sailed in from the sea one day when I was there and discharged a hundred and twenty tons of coal that she had brought down from the North. The farmers sent their carts to bring the stuff away and every cottager had a load of it.

In the back garden were huge greengage trees and a bullace, and in their shade a beehive and the ferret cage. Bert, the eldest boy, always promised me he would take me ferretting when I got older – but it never happened. There were also whisperings, half uttered and not really to be heard, of long-netting for partridges! I never got in on that. I remember once when such whisperings were going on Mr Fisher saying: 'I 'on't have any sech talk in this house!' but although his face looked strict as he said it his eyes twinkled. The vegetable garden was magnificent: I have never seen such ebullience before or since. Its fertility had three causes: the contents of the lavatory bucket were buried in it, there was a pig in a stye at the bottom of the garden, and once a year the farmer used to send a cart-load of bullock manure to be dumped over the fence.

But it was in that warm kitchen that the magic was concentrated: the strong magic of a real home! It is very hard to describe this to anyone who has not experienced it. There could never be any alienation between the generations in such a household. The home gave an assurance of security, comfort, love and contentment and anyone brought up in it could never be other than a secure and contented individual.

I compare all this in my mind with many another dwelling-place I know. We enter the house of some friends of ours in the suburb of Tatville, outside a big city. The house looks exactly like its neighbours: how could it not do because they all sprung from the same set of plans. Each has a car outside it: how could it not because the place is far from any shop, far from any pub. The planning of it presupposes a motor-car way of life. The houses look not so much ugly as undistinguished. How could they not do because they were built for the wrong purpose. They were built, not to make homes for people – that was secondary – but to make money for a property developer; the motivation was wrong. The front door, beginning to look pretty tatty now because it is ten years old, has a ridiculously-shaped design meant to look like the rising sun – or is it the setting sun. Inside, the internal doors are made of banged-together frames of unseasoned deal, clad on both sides with a material only a step up from cardboard. Cupboards and shelves are made of chipboard: wood that has been ripped to bits and stuck together again with some glue which we are told now is pretty deleterious. It may be covered with veneer to make it look like real wood but alas, after ten years of use, the veneer is beginning to peel in places and disclose what the stuff is *really* made of. The cupboards in the kitchen were not made by craftsmen but by factory hands. They will not hold screws very well and so these are beginning to come out; they have got wet so the chipboard has begun to swell and come to pieces.

The 'kitchen', or food preparation area (certainly *kitchen* is far too noble a word to be applied to it), has all the grace and charm of a third-class dentist's waiting room. Nobody would wish to spend a second longer in it than was absolutely necessary. Hence the microwave oven and the wall-mounted tin opener and all the other paraphernalia of the instant-meal culture. No wonder the food in that house – eaten at one end of the 'living room' on a shiney, cheap-and-nasty table set near the television set so that one can watch while eating – is awful. There is no proper facility for storing food – which leads to constantly having to 'pop round to the shop'.

The television screen *was*, until recently, the focus of this home. There is, indeed, a gas fire with imitation lumps of coal in it which glow when it is alight – but nobody would want to sit in front of *that*. So the family were wont to gather before the sacred screen; the only conversations allowed were arguments about which of the many 'channels' they should tune into. But even that focus is a focus no longer: the home, as a home, has now completely broken up. Each child has her or his *own* television in her or his own bedroom and the bedrooms are centrally heated. There is nothing to bring the family together now – even food tends to be snatched hurriedly at different times to suit each person's television convenience.

I am not describing an exceptional household – I am describing what is becoming the norm in Western industrial countries. Is there any wonder that true civilization is breaking down? Is there any wonder that the generations become estranged from each other, so that the parents can no longer communicate meaningfully with the children, and the latter are driven out into the streets to engage in dubious activities?

There can be no true hospitality in a house such as I have described. Even if the host has the grace to turn the television off while talking to his guests he will probably be uneasily aware that he is missing his 'favourite programme'. Generally the *sound* is turned down but the images left flickering, and what passes for conversation is conducted with the participants looking at the screen and not into one another's eyes.

I know a boy who was a superb naturalist for his age. He knew of every fox earth and badger sett in the local countryside. He could tickle a trout and gaff a salmon. And his father got him a television set. 'He's so fond of natural history,' he told me. 'I don't want him to miss the marvellous natural history programmes on the telly.' The boy is to be seen on the mountain, or in the woods, or along the streams, no longer. For who would wish to see mere badgers when they can sit at home in the warm and see *lions*?

How can we recreate the real Home? It is a goal we must achieve if our civilization is to survive. When I lived in Suffolk, and my family were young, we had no electric light and so in the evening we were almost bound to congregate under the glow of the big Aladdin lamp by the fire. We used to tell each other stories, or read books to each other, or talk and play with the children, and the home was a home. When we moved to Wales we had electric light but the only form of heating was the huge *simnai fawr*, or big fireplace. This always had some huge logs burning in it, generally it had sides of bacon or hams slung up in it to smoke, we all used to gather round it, every evening, and talk, and the neighbours would drop in, and drink home-brewed beer, and exchange local gossip, talk about the farming, and tell stories of days gone by. The teenage friends of my then teenage children would come in, and there would be singing occasionally, or music, and we used to improvise rough and ready musical groups with such instruments as we had, and young and old would join in regardless.

The Home of the future may have to be different from all that. The wood or coal guzzling fireplace may have to be a thing of the past. Much of the warmth of the house may have to come from solar power direct, or wind power, or whatever else. But our homes can still be beautiful and satisfying places.

Can I put in a plea for *craftsmanship* throughout the home? It seems to be a rule that beautiful things have been beautifully produced, and ugly articles emanate from ugly places. Go into a high-tech modern furniture factory and you will be greeted by a hell of noise, dust and ugliness. The wretched operatives have to wear face masks to keep themselves from getting lung diseases, and ear muffs to stop themselves from going deaf. Generally they are working with wood that has been destroyed by being 'chipped' and therefore has no grain or character, or if they are using undestroyed wood they are simply shoving it into extremely dangerous high speed machines that rip it into some sort of shape making an ear-splitting din as they do so. Most of the wood ends up on the floor as shavings, offcuts or sawdust. As everything is being done at high speed there is no time for careful consideration of the material, and the waste in such factories is colossal.

Compare this with the workshop of a real craftsperson. It is a quiet and peaceful place; if machine tools are used they are used with moderation and discretion: the craftsperson rules the machine not the other way round. Each article is carefully planned and designed, and the particular nature of the wood or other material being used will influence its design. Furniture made thus may last generations; it is worth caring for and therefore it *is* cared for.

The factory-made rubbish, although it may look very shiny and 'modern' in the showroom, will begin to show what it is truly made of within a dozen years. It is *tat*, fit only to be dumped in the nearest land-fill site (you mustn't burn it – it gives off dioxins). It was destined for that fate when it was knocked together and has never been anything else but three-dimensional pollution.

Ah, you may say, but there are not enough craftsmen and women to provide us with all the things that we need. This is true, but there soon would be if we encouraged the ones already working by seeking them out and buying their wares. Individual craftspeople could never supply all the furniture needed by the masses? Well do *you* consider yourself one of 'the masses'? I certainly don't. And surely furniture, or any other artefact, that will last for centuries, is a better way of providing for human needs than tat that will have to be dumped after ten years? Surely it would be better to do without this or that for a while and wait until one could afford a piece of good honest solid furniture?

You may think making furniture out of wood contributes to the destruction of the forests and the raising of the carbon dioxide level. Well, it doesn't as I explained in the chapter on energy (p.40). When an old tree is felled a young tree will grow in its place and that young tree will be very much more effective at mopping up $CO_2$. The tree that was felled, if made into furniture, will go on for ever acting as a $CO_2$ sink, unless some fool burns it or allows it to rot. Therefore the more we build good solid wooden objects the more we reduce the destruction of the atmosphere. So let us encourage the craftsperson, and even consider becoming craftspeople ourselves, for there is nothing more satisfying or more useful. Let us fill our homes with good solid honest things again and fling out the plastic rubbish.

As for the house itself – surely we must develop a different attitude to the whole business of providing ourselves with dwellings? When a young city couple makes it into the yuppy ranks and manages to keep a little of what they earn away from the tax collector, the first thing they think of is to move out into the country, or at least the commuter-belt, and look for an old house: one built long before planning laws, 'building standards', and the speculative builder, and before the natural good taste of the countryman had been corrupted and destroyed. If they can find such a dwelling they pay through the nose for it and live happily ever after. They feel they have indeed made it.

If they cannot find an old house they may very well think of building their own. Now probably the most satisfying thing a person can do during their lifetime is to design and build their own dwelling. When people try to think up solutions for all the problems in the world they arrive at feelings of complete hopelessness; but when they address themselves to solving their *own* individual problems they experience success. We cannot all live in houses which were designed and built for the occupant, you say? No, but *you* can – I can. I do. But *the masses* cannot be housed in that way? I don't believe in *the masses*, I only believe in individuals. I look forward to the day when the only people who think or talk about *the masses* will be a few dear old-fashioned Trotskyists who will coexist along with the Flat-Earthers.

At present, in many Western countries, it is made almost impossible to build your own home, or have it built for you, by stupid and restrictive planning laws. To get permission to build your own home on your own land is well-nigh impossible. And as for buying a plot of land that already has planning permission you can, unless you are very rich, forget it. An acre of agricultural land in, for example, Britain, might be worth a thousand pounds. The moment Lord Luck, in the guise of some 'planning officer', scribbles his signature on a piece of paper giving it planning permission its value jumps up very easily to two hundred times that amount – often more. At eight building plots an acre that makes £25,000 a plot, so our self-builder has got to fork out that sum before he or she even lays a brick.

Why should the owner of that acre suddenly be handed £199,000 on a plate just because some official has signed a piece of paper? And why should some young couple, desperate to build a home for themselves, be denied the right to do it by stupid and antiquated laws? Surely one of the most important of the Rights of Man should be the right to construct one's own home? Even the robin and the wren are not denied that right!

If there were no planning laws houses would spring up all over the place you say? Well, I say they would not; for if people already have houses (and most of them have) they do not need to build more houses. If people need houses then they must be allowed to build houses, it is their basic right – and without paying some huge tax to some landowner just because he has been granted 'planning permission'.

I am not saying there should be no planning laws at all. I would personally like to see it obligatory to consult the people who will be the nearest neighbours to a proposed new house to find out what their views should be. I don't think they should be able to veto the right of anyone to build their own home on their own land but they could well have a voice in the siting of such a house, appearance and other matters. Our countryside is being depopulated at the moment because young country people cannot get houses in it. The existing ones are all snapped up for holiday homes by rich city people, those who wish to build their own houses are prevented by the planning laws and hence the drift to the towns and the draining of young life from the countryside. It is time country people put what pressure they can on the people who make these stupid rules to do away with the whole tyrannical structure of the 'planning laws', and replace it with something that, somehow, gives every inhabitant of this planet the *basic right* to build his or her own house, on his or her own land.

I am not suggesting that everybody should build their own house. After all, if houses were built to last, and the population was stable, everyone should inherit an old house anyway. But I am saying that if you *can* build your own house, either with your own hands or with the help of a professional builder, it is a marvellous thing to do. Then you will really have a *home*, and it will be a real home, and you will be happy and contented. And when I enter one of the many ruined and empty farmhouses or cottages in the country where I live, I stand for a minute in silence in front of the cold and deserted *hearth*, because I am standing before a shrine.

# 7. Rubbish and Recycling

When archaeologists of the future try to make sense of this age we live in they might well name it the Rubbish Age, as we have named ages of the past 'Stone Age', and so on. For wherever they are likely to sink their spades into what were once the high-tech countries they will turn up *rubbish*. We generate more of that than the people of any former age.

Soon there will be no more possible landfill sites to dump our rubbish in. We will be forced to stop looking upon it as rubbish, and to look upon it as material which has been used once (or more) and will be used again.

Once it was the Steptoes of this world that did most of the recycling: the any-old-iron men and Raggie Jacks. Every day in most towns and cities when I was a boy one would see, in any street, at least one horse-drawn trolley rumbling along, and people would bring out for recycling anything they didn't want. Alas, it gradually became less profitable, and a pair of Gypsy scrap dealers I know told me of the day when they decided to go in for another trade. They had been reduced to carrying live goldfish with them, in plastic bags full of water; these were issued to any child who managed to persuade his mother to bring out some scrap. During one long last day of travelling – and shouting – they went back to their trailer empty-handed; they had got nothing. So they fried and ate the goldfish and that was that. We should not be too disapproving when we see a Travellers' caravan site with piles of old scrap iron or rags lying about; these people were recycling waste material long before anyone else had thought of it.

It is vitally important that we should start recycling all our waste as quickly as possible. Consider: smelting new aluminium from aluminium scrap uses 95 per cent less energy than smelting it from ore. The forests of South America are being bulldozed to make way for yet more dams to provide the electrical power to smelt aluminium ore. And yet our landfill sites are chock full of old aluminium cans that have been used once – to contain some sweet fizzy water – and then flung away.

It is said that it takes 30 gallons of oil *extra* to make a tonne of glass from the raw material than it does to recycle existing glass or *cullet*. This is a good argument for bottle banks. But I would like to see the time when bottle banks become a thing of the past – except on a small scale to collect bottles which have been broken by accident. We should *re-use* bottles. It is obviously far less damaging to our planet to re-use bottles than to crunch them up to make cullet and then melt them down again. However, the *scale* of the drinks industry makes recycling of bottles uneconomic. If you had, for example, a small brewery, and a soft drinks bottling plant (assuming we need the sweet fizzy water) in every part of the country, then it would be the easiest thing in the world to have returnable bottles. But when the stuff has to be carried hundreds of miles from some remote factory then it is far less easy and economic to return bottles. This is just one of the many real advantages of small-scale industry. Meanwhile, we should try to encourage the re-use of existing bottles as much as we can. Our traditional milk delivery service, employing re-usable bottles and electric vehicles is a highly efficient system.

As for the rather inelegantly named *putrescibles* – organic wastes that will go bad and stink if we don't do something about them – the traditional country way of recycling that was to put it through the pig in the stye at the bottom of the garden. It was thus turned into instant compost which was one of the sources of the cottage garden's great fertility. Nowadays, if we have a decent sized garden, we can bury it in the compost heap. I say bury it because if we just throw it on top it will encourage rats, cats, and your neighbour's dog. Buried it will quickly heat up and be transformed into good fertile compost in no time.

There are other things that can be done with organic waste. I have seen, in Witzenhausen in Germany, the green dustbin method. Every householder has been issued with a green dustbin, into which all organic wastes go; this is collected every so often, taken out to the nearby agricultural college's farm, and composted. The work is actually done by the students' union, which makes a handsome profit from it: the compost is bagged and sold back to the public. Everybody benefits: the municipality doesn't have to burn or dump the stuff, the gardeners can buy the compost, and the students make a profit. A few other enlightened municipalities are beginning to do the same thing, but it is a measure of the obtuseness and lack of awareness of so many of our town councillors that nobody in Britain operates such a scheme.

One great disadvantage of this method is that the composting process gives off methane gas, one of the most effective of the so-called greenhouse gases. We should not be pumping it up into the air. However, the obvious and elegant solution is to let the compost generate its methane – and then make use of it! In other words, burn it ourselves for cooking or for heating; methane is almost exactly the same as natural gas. It can be burnt quite simply by using an anaerobic digester. This is a simple tank, often nowadays made of fibre glass, into which any organic matter is dumped, the methane gas is taken off from the top by a pipe and the spent liquids and solids, now quite safe, harmless and odourless, drawn off to be used to fertilize the land. The nitrogen in the waste is fixed by this process, so that it does not waste itself into the air as ammonia gas, all phosphates and potassium and other elements useful to plants are retained, and the stuff is a most valuable fertilizer. I know a farm in Shropshire where all the cow, sheep and turkey manure goes into such a digester; the farmhouse is entirely heated for free by the gas, the liquid is piped out and sprayed onto the grass fields, and the solids are screened out and bagged and sold as garden fertilizer at a handsome profit. I have seen sheep and cows grazing the grass happily the day after the grass was sprayed – something they would never do on land sprayed with raw slurry; and the growth of grass after spraying is most dramatic.

Can I make a plea here that we should work all out for a hundred per cent of *human* sewage to be recycled in this way? It is quite absurd that we should be mining the world's dwindling reserves of phosphate and potash, dumping it on the land, consuming it in our food, and then flushing it down the sewers into the sea. It is nothing less than insane. When the deposits of phosphates and potassium are finished – and they soon will be – the world will be desperately short of these elements, for they cannot be extracted again from the ocean. This is by far the most important problem that humankind is faced with, more important, in my opinion, than the destruction of the rainforests or the greenhouse effect. We must put every pressure we can on the authorities to address this problem. The anaerobic digester is the perfect answer to the sewage disposal problem; it is the only way by which all the useful elements of sewage can be put back into the land. It can only be done, of course, if we have a dual drainage system, so that nearly all the water – and any industrial effluent – goes down one system and human sewage, with just enough water to carry it, goes down another. We have given the engineers the wrong brief. We have said get rid of it when we should have said recycle it. We must say that now.

Just as sewage should be kept apart from all the water that runs off the roofs and down the streets, so all so-called 'rubbish' must be kept separate at source. The place to start recycling is in the home. If solid rubbish is all mixed up it is almost impossible – and very expensive – to sort it out again. Every householder should have several small dustbins: one for organic waste, one for aluminium, one for non-returnable glass, one for tinned cans, and one for plastic. Plastic, by the way, is hugely overused. It hadn't been invented fifty years ago, or most of it hadn't, and the world got on surprisingly well without it. We should refuse to buy goods which are overwrapped in plastic. As far as recycling goes, by far the best solution is one that has been developed in Germany: melting it down and turning it into building panels which are strong and good insulators. Paper and rags should also be kept separate and turned in for recycling.

It should be mandatory for councils to collect all these items, separately, and see that they get recycled. Our poor suffering old planet just cannot stand the wastage and pollution of rubbish dumping any more. We owe it to our children and our children's children to put an end to this scandal: we are rifling their inheritance.

# COUNTRY AND TOWN

# 8. Country and Town

Country and town: it should always be that way round. The country was there before the town. Country people could exist without the town – not the other way round. The domination of the country by the town has for very long been an evil thing and many of the world's troubles are the result of it.

But most people in the developed world now live in towns or cities, and in developing countries, too, rural populations are falling over each other to move to the nearest big city. City life has become the norm now for most people in our world. City values and attitudes are infiltrating the country too; more and more people who live in the country are merely transplanted city people and their hearts are back on the streets and pavements.

True there is a trickle the other way now. In both Europe and North America there has been a growing current of people bucking the world trend. People, born and brought up in the city – the products perhaps of half a dozen city-bred generations – trying to get back to what they have suddenly seen as their birthright: the open countryside. Some of them made it, in the past forty or fifty years. They have managed to find, or build, homes in the country and have now become country people. But this counter-stream is drying up. The desire to move to the country is still there, if anything stronger, and in more people, but alas it is being thwarted. The would-be settlers can find nowhere to settle.

This is not because the countryside is becoming too populated: far from it. If you travel through almost any European or North American countryside you will notice that it is practically uninhabited. People, notably city people, often say 'We like it that way.' But humankind should have a place in the landscape just as trees, birds, crops, wild and domestic animals have. I can think of peopled landscapes in a score or more of countries which sing with beauty. Of course we need uninhabited wilderness too, places where the non-human world can be itself and where we humans can go and refresh our souls.

I have heard country people say: 'Thank God most people want to live in the cities! Let them stew there and leave us in peace!' I do not share this attitude. I want to see many more city people come to the country, and settle there, and bring life and new ideas and culture. I know a country culture can be swamped by too many of them and this is sad but it is not inevitable. The country where I farmed for seventeen years, and brought up my family, had practically no 'blow-ins' from elsewhere when I got there. The Welsh language culture, with its story-telling, its songs, its *nosen lawen* or choral evenings, its celebration of the Old New Year (*Hen Nos Galan*), the great swelling choruses we used to sing and the home-brewed beer we used to make – and drink – the hymns, the strange and ancient *Pwnc* ceremony which used to take place once a year in the local chapel: all this was untouched and in full vigour. Now, 27 years after I arrived there, most of this has gone. It is easy to put most of the blame for its disappearance on the newcomers from England, but there are other factors involved. The *pop* culture among the young Welsh people, the all-pervasive English-language radio and television, the cult of *Dallas*. It is not all the newcomers' fault;

they have even brought good things. They have occupied and rebuilt the deserted ruinous farmhouses and cottages, they have filled the schools which would otherwise have been closed down for lack of children (the young locals all go away) they have brought much-needed skills and professions, they organize drama groups, and choral groups, and bands, and all sorts of activities. Many of them try to learn Welsh and their children do learn it. If only there could be more good will on both sides, and determination that the new settlers be absorbed into the old culture, their arrival would be most beneficial. I would love to come back in a couple of hundred years and see the result of it all. It might not be all bad. Wales of course, like all small countries overwhelmed and dominated by huge ones, has suffered severely over many centuries from this domination. But the ingress of friendly settlers (you do not go and make your home in a country unless you love it) is not domination. It is up to the Welsh people themselves to insist that the incomers integrate, and to a certain extent this they are doing. But time, many generations, will do this job for them.

And if people wish to move to the countryside, any countryside, they should be allowed to – after all nobody stopped the rush to the cities in the nineteenth century. Why should we try to stem the flood the other way?

It is becoming more and more difficult, indeed impossible, for most young city people to move to the country.

We have dealt with the reasons for this elsewhere in this book but the two most relevant are: the price of land, and the planning laws. The first could be solved easily: by a graduated tax on land, meaning that the landowner would pay more per acre, or other unit, the more land she or he had. The second could be cured by simply rewriting the planning laws so as to give any person who owns a piece of land the right to build a dwelling on it – *and* a workshop if he or she needs one to earn a living. Of all the Rights of Man that should be the first. It would solve the problems not only of potential newcomers but of the local population too.

But meanwhile not everybody wants to go and live in the country. Most of them will no doubt continue to go on living in town. What of them? While it is true to say that the country could do without the town – it would not do very well. To milk a large herd of cows three hundred and sixty-five days every year, except leap years when the number of days is three hundred and sixty six, may seem, to some people, a satisfying life. Many country people have to do just that. Personally I should find it intolerable. As a subsistence peasant (which I have been for most of my life) I have happily milked one cow once a day (my wife milked her once a day too) and lived very well and enjoyed my life. All country people could live like that *if there were no towns*. For if there were no towns there would be no *need* for huge herds of cows to be milked, and no market for the milk anyway. There would also be no debt, few taxes, and no expenditure on town-produced goods. Dallas would be far away.

But if there were no towns there would be an absence of many other things too. There would be no chance of the bright daughter of the peasant farmer to go to university. The village school teacher might not be a very educated person. There would be no decent libraries. There would be no great orchestras. There would be no ballet, no opera; drama there might be but it would be pretty static and unsophisticated. No doubt there would be some big gains for the country people: they would discover their roots again, and rediscover their own culture: folk art, folk costume, folk dance, folk literature and folk music would all be revived, or developed. The traditions of good vernacular crafts and architecture would come back. But people would not be able to go to Dublin, like I did the other day, and see *Cats*.

I like to think that the towns could be the flowering of the countryside. I believe that Periclean Athens was just that; with its roots in the countryside around it, drawing its sustenance from there, acting as a centre of culture and scholarship for its own surrounding countryside, with most of its citizens having a base in the country too – one foot in it, as it were – it produced a great flowering of art, science and culture, tiny though it was.

I am well aware that the Atheneans had slaves. We have people living in cardboard boxes. The more's the pity. But it is my contention that a small nation *could*, if its inhabitants went about it properly, build up a high civilization without either. You do not *need* slaves to give people enough leisure to write books or compose music – any more than you need huge, earth-destroying high-tech factories. You merely need the will to live simply and tread lightly on the Earth.

Consider which cities of Europe the cultured tourist is likely to visit for inspiration and enjoyment. These cities all have one thing in common: they were originally built as the cultural centres of small city-states. I must quote here from a book called *New Politics* by John Papworth (published by Garlandfold) which has a lot to say on this subject and which, though sadly unknown to almost everybody, deserves to have world-wide readership.

To walk into the main square of Florence or Vienna is to experience to this day a profoundly moving expression of civic genius with which absolutely nothing of the modern era of meganation states can possibly compare or remotely emulate, and what those people built, and the way in which they accomplished it, for all the negative aspects of the life of the times, holds the profoundest lessons for all who are concerned to ensure that the achievements of the political process are notched up today in terms of quality, as much as of quantitatively measurable satisfactions.

The people of the city states were no less greedy, sensuous, vicious, cruel, spiteful, violent, selfish and depraved than any other time before or since. What must compel our wonder is the way in which they ordered their affairs and kept their vices in sufficient check to enable a civic life of the most matchless achievement to flower from generation to generation in a perpetually rising crescendo of splendour and loveliness which holds the mind spellbound with the richness and variety of its accomplishment.

I know that beauty is subjective, and that what I find beautiful you might find ugly. But it is surprising how many people find Florence, or the older parts of York or Carcasonne, beautiful and how few people would find beautiful most of our modern urban developments. Personally I am outraged by what I have seen in Johannesburg, Kansas City, New York, Birmingham and London. The rubbish that blows about the streets may not be very important, but it is a symptom: a symptom of a complete breakdown of civic self-respect. The human rubbish too – the junkies and the alcoholics and the pimps and the prostitutes and the layabouts and bar-flies! The obscenely rich and the utterly destitute – and the *bored*, the *bored*. If there is one suitable emblem of the modern megalopolis it is the *yawn*! It is ugly, ugly, and boring. And, as it grows, it grows further and further away from what its true function should be: to form a centre and focus of culture and civilization.

Papworth was talking of architecture only perhaps, but after all that is chiefly what has come down to us and what we notice. He could also have talked of painting and sculpture, poetry and learning. The civilizations of the small city states that he was extolling no doubt had many blemishes. The poor were no doubt very poor, the rich too rich and powerful. There were the equivalent of our junkies and alcoholics – and the pimps and the prostitutes too! But I submit: our age will leave nothing to posterity of the sumptuousness and beauty of the old part of Salzburg, or Venice, or Vienna, or Florence. The concrete-block supermarkets will be our most important legacy, and the housing estates. But this is the age of the 'Common Man' you may say. Do you wish to be a common man (or woman)? I don't.

And yet cities can be so beautiful. Cobbett, one of the few real prophets in this country, saw what was going to come when he named the London of his day the *Wen*: the sore, the cancer. He could see it coming. He could sense that the city was growing out of proportion; it was spreading its commercial tentacles too far, and losing its organic relationship with the country around it. The country which should have supported it and which it should have serviced and supplied with the good things that can only come from cities was being destroyed. The great Wens act like vortices – sucking the talented, the geniuses, the skilled out of the countryside and the provinces into the cities, and then somehow corrupting and trivializing them.

But enough of that. What can modern city people, who

want to go on living in the city, do to make things better for themselves? The first thing, I would say, would be to fight to get decisions that affect local people made by local people. The modern citizen has been disenfranchised and disempowered: decisions that affect him or her are being made further and further away. People of each street, or city parish, or group of streets, should get together and grab the power of making local decisions back into their own hands. People tend now to feel utterly helpless about this; they have sunk to the condition of giving up – they are just prepared to leave all decisions that affect them or their locality to some 'them' far away. We must make 'them' redundant. We must sack Nanny. We must walk out of the nursery and start making decisions about things that affect us ourselves.

Meanwhile may I make a suggestion that I believe would benefit enormously people of both country and town? Why not every city person try to establish a link with some particular country person? And vice versa. There could be house swapping, so that the city person could get to stay, cheaply, in the country sometimes and the country person could have the benefit of town visits. There could be an exchange of goods and services. All farmers are desperately short of labour, and all city people could benefit greatly by doing some manual work from time to time, in the fresh air. I used to have inner city children come for holidays on my farm in Wales from time to time.

On occasions I have bought 'scrap' hens from battery cage operators. When you let them out in the open at first they fall over when they try to stretch their wings: they have never been able to do it in their lives. They look pathetic when they are trying to learn to walk, for the first time ever. They gradually learn to scratch the ground for worms or earwigs or whatever. It takes them a week to learn to be hens.

The city kids who used to come to my farm reminded me of them.

# THE LAND, FARMING
## AND FOOD

# 9. The Land

Except in so far as we eat a little fish, and less seaweed, we humans are creatures of the soil. A person living in the middle of Manhattan, or Tokyo, is a soil organism just as an earthworm is. And, as Jacks and Whyte wrote in a book called *The Rape of the Earth* in 1939: 'Below that thin layer comprising the delicate organism known as the soil is a planet as lifeless as the moon.' If the soil goes we all go: let there be absolutely no doubt about that. There is no future for our species if we destroy the soil.

For ten thousand years people have ploughed and dug this Earth. And wherever they have done it moderately and rationally they have preserved its fertility and its productiveness. Where they have been too rapacious though they have destroyed the soil, and this is not only a modern phenomenon.

The first arable farmers are thought to have existed in the quarter of a million square miles of once fertile land in the north of the countries now known as Iraq, Eastern Turkey and the high country in the north-west of Persia. Some archaeologists look upon this area as the Garden of Eden. For many millennia it was closely inhabited by Stone Age farming people and – if they had been left alone – their descendants would be farming there today.

But they were not left alone. For a new civilization sprang up in the south, a big city civilization, the first one ever to have existed on this planet. The Sumerian people who built it had discovered irrigation, and were able to irrigate the great flat desert area watered by the Tigris and Euphrates rivers, and there is not the slightest doubt that it was the weight of those great cities that destroyed the soil of the Garden of Eden country in the north.

City people conquer country people. The citizens of the south stripped the forests from the hills of the north to provide wood to burn to make bricks for their cities. This caused soil erosion, and a quarter of a million square miles of what was perhaps the most fertile country in the world was stripped of topsoil and rendered into the almost uninhabited desert that it is today. As for the irrigated land of the south – Mesopotamia – that was rendered completely sterile by salination, the curse of all irrigation farmers in hot dry climates. I have been to both those countries and have seen what happened there. I have seen the myriad *tells* – hills that were once villages – in the now uninhabited lands of the north, and have stood on the ziggurat of Uruk, one of the mighty cities of the south – and looked out over miles of salt-encrusted desert and thought about the mutability of humankind.

I have travelled over the western Great Plains of North America, the present bread basket of the world, and seen the sad remains of an agricultural civilization that lasted just fifty years, wiped out by the dust bowl debacle in the 1930s. I have seen galloping water-borne soil erosion in the eastern Great Plains area where the rainfall is too high for wind erosion. I have revisited areas in east and central Africa, which I knew well before the Second World War, and have witnessed the cancer of erosion: savage gulleys that become enlarged with every rainy season; nobody knows what to do about it. There is sheet erosion that leaves isolated stones perched up on pillars of soil, starving cattle and hungry children.

But let no one accept the testimony of one man on a subject as shatteringly important as this one. As early as the 1930s, when the wind-borne erosion of the dust bowl was raging further west, the Missouri Experimental Station began research into water-borne erosion. It found that whereas land in maize-wheat-clover rotation, with cattle to add manure to the soil, was losing 2.7 tons of topsoil per acre per annum, land on stockless farms with maize monoculture was losing 19.7 tons per acre per annum (Bulletin 366. Missouri Experimental Station, 1936).

At the International Conference on Soil Erosion held in Honolulu in 1983, the following figures for annual loss of soil were given:

| Region | Soil Loss (tonnes per hectare) |
| --- | --- |
| Texas | 40 |
| Colorado | 32 |
| Iowa | 30 |
| Baltic Sea Region of USSR | 59 |
| Rostov | 46 |
| Transcaucasia | 32 |

The United States Aid Mission to Ethiopia reported in 1978: 'There is an environmental nightmare unfolding before our eyes . . . over one billion tons of topsoil flow from Ethiopia's highlands each year.' The report goes on to say that the tree cover of the highlands had been reduced from 40 per cent of the area to 7 per cent since the country had achieved independence in 1941. That, and mechanized farming, had caused the destruction of the soil.

According to the American Society of Agronomy, which is based at Madison, Wisconsin (report published in 1982), the *sediment load* of the Yellow River in China, which drains 668,000 square kilometres, is 1,600 million tonnes of soil per annum. The Ganges (which drains 1.1 million square kilometres) carries 1,455 million tonnes per annum, the Mississippi carries 300 million tonnes per annum.

A report of the Iowa State University Experimental Station (*Our Thinning Soil*, February 1977) says:

> The 200 million tons of soil lost from Iowa's croplands each year, for example, simply cannot be replaced within our lifetimes or those of our children. The eroded soil has gone, depleting the fertility of the land.

The same story can be told in every country in the world. The soil is going. Even cosy little England, with its mild temperate climate is beginning to lose its soil. According to Bob Evans, of the Soil Survey of England and Wales, East Anglia – our main corn belt – is losing eighteen tonnes of soil from each hectare every year. And what is the reason for this? Why are so many areas of this planet, which have been continuously farmed for four or five thousand years with no loss of soil, suddenly galloping down into the nearest river, or blowing away, like the Black Earth steppes of Russia and western Great Plains in the United States?

Here is a quotation from Worldwatch Paper 24. (The Worldwatch Institute is by no means some sort of 'green' organization intent on promoting organic agriculture, or 'far-out' things like that. It is a very staid body of scientists there to advise the United States government):

> The transition to continuous cropping has been abetted by cheap nitrogen fertilizers that replaced nitrogen-fixing legumes. While these chemical fertilizers can replace nutrients lost through crop removal, they cannot make up for the loss of topsoil needed to maintain a healthy soil structure.

That is to say there is no soil erosion on organically rich soil! If there is enough *humus*, which is the soil scientist's word for decaying organic matter, the particles of soil are held together and the soil is subject neither to wind nor to water erosion. When the American settlers moved into the dry western Great Plains in the last two decades of the nineteenth century, they put the plough into it and began to reap the benefit of thousands of years of prairie grasses and the dung of countless buffalo: the land was rich in humus. They got, in spite of the dry climate, fair crops of wheat. As a result they were able to indulge in continuous wheat cropping. It was in the year 1929 that the citizens of New York went out of their doors one windy morning and found half an inch of dust on the streets. It was the topsoil of the western Great Plains which was blowing away. The humus in that soil was all used up; the farmers did not replace it because they kept no cattle and so grew no grass, alfalfa or clover; there was no organic matter to plough back into the soil. The soil had become a sterile dust which blew away. Steinbeck wrote his great novel *The Grapes of Wrath* about the plight of the wretched settlers who had ruined a vast tract of country in one generation.

To me it is fitting that the citizens of New York should have seen the direct results of this catastrophe – for it was they and their like who had caused it! It is the insatiable demands of the great cities more than anything else that destroy the soils of our planet. Imperial Rome destroyed the lowland soils of Italy, and then turned to North Africa for its grain. If you want to see the enormous granaries they built there you have to dig them out of the sand dunes of the desert they created. Knossos destroyed the topsoil of Crete – and destroyed itself by doing so. As we have seen, the cities of the Sumerians – the first cities in the world – turned their own countryside into a salt desert and caused the destruction of the highlands to the north. Mohenjodaro, in Pakistan, was contemporaneous with Ur. I have stood among its ruins looking out at a desert land.

And now arable farmers all over the world are practising the same sort of get-rich-quick monoculture. They are able to do this because they can replace lost nutrients from the fertilizer bag, and keep the debilitated crops that result from this sort of farming alive with constant dousings of pesticides. They too, if we let them, will ruin the land in a generation.

What has all this got to do with the probable readership of this book? As only 2 per cent of the population of many industrialized countries is connected with the land one might answer 'not very much'. Well I submit it has everything to do with every one of us. You are a soil organism too! You need the topsoil as much as the farmer. This is a problem that we absolutely *have* to solve if we are to survive. We cannot just leave this to the farmers, or the experts, or the government, or even to the Lord God above. We have got to tackle it – each and every one of us – ourselves. The future of our world depends on it.

Living in north-western Europe, or on the eastern seaboard of the United States, one might be forgiven for not being very worried about soil erosion. Permanent grassland does not erode, or at least if it does it does not erode faster than new soil formation, and there is a lot of permanent grassland in these areas. Further, there are still the remains of a tradition of good husbandry, and farmers will put land down to temporary grass and clover leys, then plough these up again, thus returning that organic matter into their soil. Also, in a temperate climate with an evenly-spaced rainfall, erosion is less prevalent. But even in these areas soil erosion is becoming serious. White straw monoculture in Europe, and maize monoculture in the eastern United States are beginning to take their toll. East Anglian farmers have no *right* to lose eighteen tonnes of topsoil per hectare per year. They are cheating their descendants out of their birthright.

The so-called 'Green Revolution' of the nineteen sixties was an ecological disaster. Tropical farmers were persuaded to use short-strawed, high-yielding, nitrate-hungry hybrid crops. The seed came as part of a package: mechanization and chemicalization were the other parts of it, and another very important component was *debt*. The farmers had to desert their age-old practices, which had maintained the fertility of their soils for millennia, in order to go in for monocultural cash-cropping. Animals were phased out to allow of this and their dung – the most valuable substance on this Earth – was no longer returned to the soil. Further, only the richer farmers were able to take 'advantage' of this marvellous 'new deal'. The poorer peasants went out of business and their holdings were swallowed up by the rich farmers who were able to adapt to the new methods. But above all *the land* suffered. For the new high-yielding hybrids would not yield at all without massive doses of nitrate and further pesticides. Monoculture of course always encourages disease. Nothing suits a disease organism, or a pest, better than having its host species growing year after year on the same land.

So part of the 'Green Revolution' package was unlimited, and very expensive, pesticides, and the land was poisoned, the crops were poisoned – and so were the people too. The two thousand people killed by the leakage of chemicals at Bhopal were the lucky ones. The tens of thousands who were ruined and blinded are the ones paying the real price.

# 10. Agrochemicals

Agrochemicals – fertilizer, pesticides, herbicides and the like – are essential to modern industrial farming. These have to be manufactured – you can't have 'em unless somebody makes 'em! – and wherever there are pesticide factories there is pollution. The Black Forest in Germany is being destroyed by acid rain caused by the chemical industry around Strasbourg. The Rhine is now a stinking chemical sewer thanks to pollution from, amongst other things, agrochemical manufacture; such fish as are still hanging on to life in its lower reaches are cancerous and diseased and nobody is allowed to eat them. The Humber, the Mersey, the Severn estuary, every great estuary in the world that has a chemical industry on its banks is grossly polluted. Our lakes, our rivers, our forests and our seas are being slowly poisoned by the chemical industry.

But we must not blame the chemical manufacturers. For if we wish to farm our world with chemicals then we must not grumble if people make chemicals. To have a polluted world is simply the price we have to pay for the benefit, if it is a benefit, of chemical farming. Factories which produce pesticides produce huge quantities of poisonous effluents: liquid, gaseous and solids. The solids may go into landfill sites, the gases are let out into the air, and the liquids eventually find their way into the water. There is absolutely nothing else that can happen to them.

So it is no good blaming the chairman of ICI. We ask for

chemicals: we cannot grumble if they are produced. You may object that *you* do not ask for them. No, but if you do ask for the food that is grown with them you are doing exactly the same thing. There is also a popular myth that we could not feed the present population of the world if we did not use agro-chemicals. Well we could, but it would mean that we would have to get more humans back on the land. The most important thing that chemicals do is to replace labour; by far the best pesticide that has ever been invented is a hoe, but it needs a man or woman at one end of it. There are plenty of new-style organic farmers in the world today who are producing yields of food crops quite comparable with those produced with chemicals.

But before we start either damning or praising agricultural chemicals, let us first find out what they are. There are two main classes of them: fertilizers and biocides. We will discuss fertilizers first.

*Nitrate* is by far the most important chemical fertilizer. The gas nitrogen makes up a vast part of the air of this planet, but it is in a free mixture with oxygen, carbon dioxide, argon and a few other gases. In global terms it is in unlimited supply. It is absolutely essential for the growth of both plants and animals – but the higher forms of animals and plants cannot make use of it. Wise old Gaia, as the living mantle of this planet has been called, got around this difficulty by evolving or creating bacteria which *can*. Some of these live free in the soil, some in symbiosis with certain higher plants and some in the guts of animals. These bacteria *fix* nitrogen by turning it into a compound with oxygen in the form of nitrate. The latter is soluble and can be taken up by higher plants. This source of available nitrogen kept the living world going until humans learned to fix nitrogen directly from the air with electrical power, and thus 'artificial' nitrate was born.

There had actually been a huge supply of high quality nitrate on the Earth before this: the deposits of sea-bird guano on the desert coast of Chile. Half the big sailing ships in the world were employed in transporting this stuff to Europe and North America to be dumped on the land. After three or four decades it was finished, and artificial nitrate came just in time to take its place.

Nitrate on the land has several effects, not all of them benign. It stimulates plant growth dramatically, particularly growth of green leaves and grain. But used in excess it causes plants to become what old-fashioned farmers called *nesh* – that is sappy and tender and open to infection by pests and disease. The inorganic farmer counters this by zapping the disease organisms with biocides. Nitrates suppress the nitrogen-fixing bacteria in the soil, so that when you use it you deny yourself this free source of nitrate.

People say it 'burns up' the organic matter in the soil. In fact it stimulates the putrefactive bacteria, which decompose organic matter very quickly, so that the matter is mineralized and disappears. It makes it possible to farm without organic manure, and as the latter is labour-intensive farmers tend to do without it. Thus the soil becomes devoid of organic matter and is liable to erosion; it is on soils heavily dosed with artificial nitrate that the worst erosion occurs. The soil becomes merely an inert and sterile powder which holds crops up while you feed them artificially.

Turned into *nitrite* in the guts of people or animals nitrate becomes a poison and causes cancer. It has recently been found to be grossly polluting to ground water. It takes several decades to sink down through the rock to the underground water. If we stopped using it now it would still be thirty or forty years before the ground water would be fit to drink because the nitrate (and assorted pesticides) are still in the rock. This phenomenon has been named 'the nitrate time-bomb'.

The various 'organic' organizations about the world will not countenance the use of inorganic nitrate. Personally I can see nothing wrong with its moderate use for special purposes, such as, for example, stimulating one field on a grassland farm to grow early in the spring and provide 'an early bite' for cattle or sheep. But modern agribusiness farmers grossly abuse it by dumping on far too much too often. It has come to take the place of good husbandry.

*Phosphate and Potash* are the two other main constituents of artificial fertilizer. Used in moderation on grassland phosphate encourages clover, which is a nitrogen-fixing plant and therefore its use makes the farmer less dependent on bought nitrate. The trouble with both these fertilizers is that, worldwide, they are in very short supply, and we cannot create them synthetically. When the phosphate and potash deposits of the world are exhausted, farming on this planet will come more or less to a stop. As I have explained elsewhere, we must start recycling human sewage; then we will achieve a cyclical use of them, not linear. At the moment we are mining them, growing food with them, eating the food, and then flushing them down the sewers into the ocean from which they will never, in any imaginable period of time, be recovered.

*Lime* is a substance in almost unlimited supply that 'sweetens' sour land: in other words neutralizes acidity. It encourages clovers in grassland and as far as I know has no deleterious effect. But soil that is well supplied with organic manure, such as composted straw and animal dung, needs far less of it.

Now we come to the other great family of agro-chemicals: the *biocides*. These, by definition, kill life.

Many plants create their own insecticides. Tobacco is one example; it creates nicotine which kills the insects which try to eat it. Pyrethrum, which we make from the flower of a daisy, is another. Derris another. These three were used by farmers and gardeners for many years before modern synthetic biocides were invented. Arsenic and cyanide, and metals such as copper and tin, have also been used as biocides.

By the last decades of the nineteenth century chemists had learned to synthesize complicated organic com-pounds. A *chlorinated hydrocarbon*, DDT, was discov-ered then in 1874, and by the late 1930s was being widely used as an insecticide. It was not until the 1960s that it was discovered to be a potent carcinogen and millions of cancers throughout the world were attributed to it. It was banned in the United States immediately and most civil-ized countries followed. Incredibly Great Britain did not ban it mandatorily until 1984! (But Britain has always been the last nation to ban any poison.) DDT is still produced on a vast scale in the industrialized world to sell to the Third World, the inhabitants of which presumably don't matter. Being fat soluble it is taken up by the fat of animals in the food chain and retained until the animal dies. It becomes more and more concentrated as it goes up the food chain (so that even the penguins of Antarctica now have it in their fat). It presents itself in mothers' milk and many American mothers were told to stop nursing their babies because of DDT poisoning.

Hydrocarbons are compounds of hydrogen and carbon

atoms. Compounds with carbon in them can be incredibly complex, owing to the power of the carbon atom to combine in so many ways, and it is these compounds which are called *organic*, for they are the stuff of Life. It is possible to replace one or more of the hydrogen atoms with atoms of chlorine to produce a huge range of poisons. The history of each seems to follow a pattern. It takes four or five years to prove that it is 'entirely harmless' to humans by testing it on rabbits and other small rodents. It then takes from fifteen to thirty years of use to find out that it is in fact toxic to humans. The more enlightened countries then ban it (Britain always comes last) but it is still manufactured for sale to the Third World.

Various isomers of hexachlorocyclohexane (HCH) followed, the best known of this family perhaps being Lindane. All the HCH group are terribly persistent in the environment, are especially destructive to fish and birds of prey. They have been shown to cause cancer in animals, and leukaemia, liver and kidney damage, and nervous disorders in humans. They have been banned in many European countries now, the United States, New Zealand and Australia are considering bans, but in the United Kingdom you can buy Lindane, the most dangerous of the HCHs, in any garden shop. The story of Aldrin, Dieldrin, Endrin and Telodrin is much the same.

The other great family of organic biocides is the *organophosphates*. These are less persistent in the environment than the chlorinated hydrocarbons, but more poisonous. They were first developed as a nerve gas for warfare. They can enter humans via the skin or as a vapour. Many of them are restricted in industrialized countries (*even* Britain!) but they are all freely available in the Third World. A survey in Brazil found that six out of ten farmers there are severely affected by organo-phosphates. A committee of experts of the World Health Organization in 1972 found that 9,000 deaths had been reported worldwide from the use of pesticides and that at least half a million people had lost their health because of them. Since then the use of pesticides has doubled.

One could fill a book with the names alone of the organic pesticides which have been developed since the Second World War. New ones come on the market every year, as the pests the older ones were aimed at develop resistance. Insects breed quickly and are incredibly adept at breeding in resistance to poisons. This means greater quantities of pesticides are used. Wheat in the United Kingdom is now sprayed up to eight times a year with different poisons, fruit trees up to ten or even a dozen times during the growth of the crop to produce that blemish-free appearance beloved of the supermarket shopper. Personally I would rather have the odd insect bite on an apple than persistent and cumulative poisons.

And what of the losses and gains of this pull-devil-pull-baker race between the chemist and insect pests? Well, according to the 1980 *Annual Review of Entomology*, (Vol.25), insects and weeds were then reducing crop yields by 30 per cent – and that was *exactly the same* as they were doing before the 'chemical revolution'! In other words the chemists and farmers have been running to stay in the same place!

And what is the alternative? Well, a large and growing number of farmers in Europe and North America are growing perfectly good crops, with yields comparable to those of chemical farmers, without any pesticides at all. They have managed to get off the pesticide treadmill altogether. They have done it by adapting the principles of good husbandry which were developed over the centuries, and bringing in new methods where appropriate; they are part of the new and growing movement of organic farmers and growers. I have seen dozens of such farms now, in Europe and North America, and they work: many of them produce yields which are over the national average, with zero inputs of chemicals.

Entomologists in the United States have developed a system of pest control which they call Integrated Pest Management (I.P.M.) They have recognized, at last, that the war against insects cannot ever be 'won' by chemicals. But successful I.P.M. requires knowledge and skill. The entomologist is called in, he assesses the situation, he may recommend just patience – suffering the damage for a little while until a predator population builds up; he may decide to bring in artificially reared predators (very effective bacterial cultures may be part of this); he may advise the farmer to intercrop another year with plants of another species, or to plant, perhaps, earlier. (When I plant my broad beans in the autumn I get no black fly damage – if I plant in the spring I do.) As a last resort he may recommend a biocidal spray. 'Calendar spraying' is anathema to him (the spraying of poisons just because the manufacturer or agricultural adviser tells you it is the right time of the year to do so). If, by observation, thought and intelligence, you can minimize pest damage without resort to poisons then you should do so.

Fifty years ago organo sprays were first used against Colorado Beetle on potatoes in North America. Crops still have to be sprayed ten times a year at a cost of $700 per hectare and yet the damage being done by the pest is undiminished. The members of the Amish community, who allow themselves no sprays at all, grow very good crops of potatoes.

But what were the reasons for this sudden massive reliance on poisons? First, monoculture – the growing of the same crop year after year on the same land – of course this favours the pest or disease, as even a child could see it must. Second, over-reliance on artificial nitrate. Crops are driven on to huge yields by this but at the expense of pest and disease resistance. Third, the breeding of crop varieties, generally hybrids, which produce huge yields in response to large applications of nitrate. Hardiness is always sacrificed for this end. Fourth, farming without organic manure. Organically rich soil grows healthy and hardy and disease-resistant crops.

Fifth, the divorcing of the animal kingdom from the vegetable one. The American farmer and writer Wendell Berry has said: 'They have taken a solution and cut it neatly down the middle into two problems.' The solution was the age-old one – as old as life itself – of the animal and vegetable kingdoms coexisting and interacting, the one providing nourishment for the other. The two problems created are: 1. how to fertilize, and retain the health of the living soil after the animals have gone away from it, and: 2. how to dispose of the manure from the animals, which instead of being the most valuable stuff on this planet – the base of all real soil fertility and health – has now become a stinking embarrassment, ending up as raw slurry in the nearest river, poisoning the fish.

We must unite the two great Kingdoms of Life again, as they have been united since the beginning of Life on this planet.

# 11. The Animal Kingdom

When I was a boy I worked on various farms in England, and thereafter on farms in South Africa and what is now known as Namibia. Having been brought up in a non-farming household I was concerned at first at what seemed to me to be an over-robust way of treating farm animals. I remember being horrified by having to hold piglets while they were being castrated – but I was partly reassured by the fact that the moment I put a piglet down he was rooting around gobbling up the bits that had been cut off him. Obviously we were hurting the piglets – but within minutes of the operation they were acting quite normally. I began to realize that I might have been indulging in anthropomorphism: I was imagining that the piglets felt and suffered in exactly the same way as I would have done under the same circumstances.

After a time I discovered that the old country people, although quite ruthless when it came to such matters as castration, or docking lambs' tails, or even slaughtering animals, in fact had a kind of rough kindliness towards them. They would never *needlessly* hurt an animal. They knew that the exigencies of earning their living in the way they did made some transient cruelty necessary, and they also knew that if there were to be pigs at all then it was necessary to control their numbers because there were no other predators to do so. If it was cruel for a man to kill a pig, then it was also cruel for a lion. They had not moved so far away from the natural world that they failed to realize that.

But now, since those pre-Second World War days, there has been a complete transformation in the way that country people look upon animals. Previously, the domestic animal was looked upon as something useful to humans, in fact essential to their existence, but it was also looked upon as a creature that had needs and demands and even a dignity of its own. Country men and women would treat their farm animals with real affection. I remember, as a boy, I had lazily neglected to perform one of my tasks, which was to put new straw bedding in the bullock yard. Bill, the old farm foreman, came along.

'Would *you* like to sleep in that?' he asked me.

'Well – no.'

'Then don't expect them things to either,' he said. He called the animals 'things', but he wasn't going to have them ill-treated.

A few years ago I went, as part of a film crew, to a modern 'beef lot' in Italy. It was near Isola Della Scala, on the flat fertile plain of the Po Valley. On 37 acres of land there were twelve huge sheds and each shed contained between 500 and 600 cattle. They had not been castrated because they were destined to make 'bull beef'; this means they are fed on a very high diet and allowed no exercise during the eighteen months they spend in there. They cannot walk about; they stand on slats – steel strips set fairly wide apart so that the shit can easily fall through. They are standing very uncomfortably and to lie down (which very few of them do since there is no room) must be a penance. Electrified wires are over their heads to stop them mounting each other – a thing cattle frequently do. These ones soon learn not to.

They are looked after by eleven labourers and five vets. The latter are there to keep them constantly under observation, for they spend their short lives under severe stress. One of the vets tells me that they are kept heavily sedated. During our afternoon's filming there I heard not one *moo* out of just under six thousand animals – although there was an occasional very disturbing *scream*.

Nobody knows what cattle feel like and it is no good imagining that they feel exactly like we would under the same circumstances, but it was obvious to me that those bulls were suffering from the most acute sensory deprivation. I have kept cows for decades and know how they behave when kept under conditions that are not too far removed from the conditions for which nature intended them. They enjoy coming into warm straw yards in the worst of the winter – but they enjoy even more being let out to pasture in the spring! They run and gambol and frisk like children let out of school! They seem to relish the sun on their backs and although the rain and the flies may annoy them they have been evolved to endure these inconveniences. They have great mother love for their calves, and they make real friendships with each other. They develop a strong hierarchical structure within the herd, which they hate being separated from. They respond touchingly to human affection.

Those bulls in the beef lot have absolutely no chance during their lives to experience any of these bovine joys. They just stand, drugged into a stupor, eat, and wait. The five vets watch them closely and medicate them constantly as occasion arises. I will not talk about the cruelty or otherwise of the two systems of keeping cattle, the old or the new; I know what I think myself. But the *ecological* differences are without question.

The *dung* from the beef lot animals dropped through the slats into water-filled channels, and was transported down to what has been euphemistically named a *lagoon*. No, do not imagine sapphire-blue waters in verdant surroundings. This one was simply a huge lake created by bulldozing up an earthen bund around its perimeter. It was filled to overflowing with some of the most disgusting stuff I have ever seen or smelt. The one friendly vet who spoke French, and was much more forthcoming than the Manager of the place, told me that the seeping of the liquids from this morass had polluted the underground water so that for many miles around it is now unfit to drink. And the far-away agribusinesses that grow the maize to feed all these animals have to put expensive and polluting artificial fertilizer on their land because they have no animal manure. As Berry said – the solution turned into two problems.

On traditional farms the animals are spread far and wide over the countryside, they are fed with the crops grown locally and they manure the fields that grow the crops. When people who do not approve of the farming of animals produce such arguments as 'It takes ten calories of energy in the form of animal feed to produce one calorie in the form of milk or meat,' they forget the most important product of all: manure, the real fertility or *heart* of the land. That is where the other nine calories go, and they are the most important.

I could describe very vividly other intensive lifestock units: pig 'sweatshops' where the pigs are kept in total darkness except for twenty minutes three times a day when the automatic feeders feed them; chained sow units where the mother sows cannot even turn round to look at the piglets they have produced; battery hen units where hens with wing spans of 21 inches are allowed four inches of cage space per bird; deep litter 'broiler' houses where the living walk over the bodies of the dead and dying because the youth in charge hasn't had time to remove the cadavers. I could go on, but I will not – I will merely ask any reader who may wish to change her or his lifestyle for the better to *go and look* at such places.

It is instructive to follow the history of the treatment of one species of farm animal over the last fifty or sixty years in order to try to understand how the sort of practices I have mentioned came about. Domestic pigs, in medieval times, were looked upon as woodland animals and were allowed to roam semi-wild in the woods. In the Domesday Book constant mention is made of *pannage* – this denoted an area of woodland large enough to feed a certain number of pigs. The pigs had to be kept alive with tail-corn and other produce throughout the spring and summer, but then, with the fall of acorns, beech mast, ash keys and other tree fruit in the autumn, they flourished and waxed fat, and the surplus was killed off and salted down into bacon.

With the coming of the pheasant craze the pigs had to be taken out of woodland, for the most part, and then the sows were very often kept in moveable shelters out on the fields, for a sow will get a fifth of her nourishment from grassland alone, and with an animal as expensive to feed as a pig this is a big consideration. The practice of *ringing* sows (putting metal rings in their noses) came in to stop them from rooting up and damaging the pasture.

Now a sow, given some freedom, exhibits a certain pattern of behaviour before she has her babies. For some days before this happy event you will see her carrying bunches of straw about in her mouth, running excitedly here and there, starting to make a nest, then thinking better of it and picking it all up and carrying it off somewhere else. If you leave a sow alone at this stage she will, almost without exception, have her complete litter peacefully and unaided, and look after them. For twenty-five years I was never without six sows kept like this, so I know what I am talking about. I hardly *ever* lost a piglet, and they suffered no disease.

Since the Second World War, as labour priced itself out of the market on farms (God knows it was priced low enough already!) farmers began to get greedy, and to listen to the bad advice poured into their ears, by the agricultural press and the 'government advisers', to *specialize*. So those that wanted to stay in pigs got more pigs, and to save the labour of feeding them they began to keep them indoors most of the time, and just let them run out onto restricted areas. Result: a build-up of pig parasites on the bare earth of the restricted areas. So the farmers kept the pigs inside all the time, on straw. Result: the sows became disturbed and upset when they were farrowing and didn't do the job properly, often smothering some piglets in the straw. So the farmer removed the straw and henceforth the sows had to farrow on bare concrete. This muddled and disturbed the sows ever further – they *must* go through their ritual of nest-making if they are to farrow naturally and easily. A *farrowing rail*, a horizontal bar to stop the sow overlaying her piglets, was put around the sow stall. But the sows, still thwarted and muddled and denied the exercise of their natural chain of instincts, continued to overlay their piglets and even eat them. So the pig farmer began to be present at the farrowing; this disturbs sows even more, and *more* piglets were killed. The infra-red lamp was introduced so that the piglets, lured by its warmth, moved away from the mum. This even more disturbed the poor old sow. (The piglets, by the way, had to have iron injected into them soon after they were born because, denied access to the earth, they became short of this element.)

However, even with farrowing rails and infra-red lights (or because of them) the sows became more and more disturbed and would get at their progeny and savage them, or lay on them, and generally exhibit unporcine behaviour. So the *farrowing crate* was introduced, and in some instances the short tethering chain. The sows were completely immobilized, like lunatics in a straight-jacket, so that they could not lay on their piglets (which more and more often were hauled out of her by the farmer), could not eat them; in fact could not even see them. There seems to me to be a certain lack of imagination in someone who makes an animal have babies and yet never ever allows her even to *look* at them even once, in her lifetime.

Of course early weaning then takes place, because the farmer can make more money like that. Using injections often forces the sow to take the boar (or the artificial insemination syringe) even earlier, so having more piglets and making more money for the farmer. The early-weaned piglets are imprisoned, each in a separate cage, so that they cannot see each other, and have absolutely no trace of the social life that this most sociable of all animals normally enjoys. They are fed on milk substitute, and high protein food (which incidentally often includes the ground-up remnants of other pigs, *or* of sheep, which might or might not have brain disease) and in due course their miserable lives are brought to an end with an electric shock and that is an end of them.

The final obscenity is the *minimal disease herd*. Piglets

produced in the conditions I have described suffer from all sorts of diseases, of course. They have no natural immunity or resistance to diseases, particularly pulmonary disease. Normally they are kept alive by constant dosings with antibiotics, but some farmers have tried to get round this by not allowing the piglets to come in contact with any source of infection whatever. To achieve this they bring the sow into a completely sterile operating theatre, kill her, and have the piglets removed from her womb by a vet. The piglets are then supposed to form the foundation of a new disease-free herd. I knew a man in Suffolk who had managed to build up a herd of four hundred sows like this, at huge expense, and then the whole lot got swine fever and had to be destroyed. I was absolutely *delighted* when I heard the news. The pigs were happier dead, and the owner got what he deserved.

Well where do we go from here? What further depths of cruelty and obscenity must we reach to satisfy an apparently insatiable lust for money and more money? We have ceased to accord our farm animals any *respect*. We have ceased to regard them as creatures having any rights of their own: they are now merely considered as *food conversion units*.

There is absolutely no need to treat living creatures in this way. Animals kept for meat can have happy and natural lives (they don't need *much* to keep them happy) until they are killed instantly and humanely; not in some huge disgusting abattoir a hundred miles away, but as near to where they have lived as possible. They have got to die some day, just as we do; and if we didn't eat pig meat, there would be no pigs left today. Belatedly, of course, outraged Nature is beginning to lash back. She is outraged, not by Mad Cow Disease, but by Mad Man Disease, for the second caused the first.

# 12. The Organic Alternative

When I was fifteen years old I started work on a farm in Essex. The year was 1930. The great chemical revolution in agriculture was just beginning to get into its stride. But Mr Catt, the farmer I worked for, hadn't joined it. He did not use any artificial fertilizer whatever, nor did he use any biocides. He didn't need them. He never grew less than two tonnes of wheat to the acre and he told me that in his opinion that was enough.

He had never heard of 'organic agriculture' – indeed I doubt if the term had been invented then. He was simply an old-fashioned traditional farmer, and he maintained the fertility of his farm by the tried methods of good husbandry. For one thing, he rotated his crops. He once told me that to grow the same crop on the same land year after year was a sin against the Holy Ghost. His rotation was: Winter Wheat, Mangolds, Spring Corn (barley and oats undersown with clover), Clover. The clover was ploughed up after yielding a crop of hay, and in went wheat again.

The only *inputs* that went into that farm from the outer world while I was there were seventy 'store' (thin) bullocks and a ton of linseed cake – a by-product of the linseed oil industry. Mr Catt said it put 'a bloom' on the cattle. The bullocks came in in the autumn and went out, fat, in the spring. The wheat he sold, and the straw (which I believe he valued more than the wheat), went as bedding in the covered yards for the bullocks. They turned it, with their dunging and treading, into what Mr Catt told me was 'the most valuable stuff in the world – more valuable than gold or diamonds'. The mangolds were fed to the bullocks, they were his 'cleaning crop'. Being a row crop they could be horse-hoed and hand-hoed, and they were why his farm was fairly free of weeds. The oats went to the horses, of which there were five, huge Suffolk Punches. There was no tractor. The barley went to my bullocks (I called them mine because it was my job to look after them); so did the oat straw and the barley straw. The *chaff* from the threshing of all the corn went to both horses and bullocks. The clover hay was mostly supposed to go to the horses but I used to pinch some of it for 'my' bullocks. The two horsemen used to retaliate by pinching some of my linseed cake. An old-fashioned horseman would starve to death rather than pinch an egg for himself or his family – but he would go to any length to steal for his horses!

The nitrogen requirement of the farm was derived, quite 'free', from the clover and the nitrogen-fixing bacteria in the guts of the animals. Mr Catt once told me that if he had dumped sulphate of ammonia on his land, not only would he have had to pay for it, but he would have grown more wheat but had to cope with disease. As it was I saw no sign of any disease, or serious pest damage, on any of his crops. The burgeoning fertility of the farm came from hundreds of tons of that stuff 'more valuable than gold or diamonds'. If Mr Catt and his successors had gone on farming like that, the farm would have maintained its health and fertility until the end of the world.

I visited the farm again in 1987. It was hard to find it; that countryside which had been so beautiful 57 years before had been turned into a vast, hedgeless, ditchless, treeless almost uninhabited barley prairie. Mr Catt's farm had been shoved together into an 800 acre holding, owned by a London finance company, tenanted by two brothers. They employed one man. What has happened to the other *seven* farmers – and the men who worked for them?

Mr Catt, on his 100 acres, had employed five besides me. If his neighbours did roughly the same that means that the 800 acres of which the farm is now a part would have given a living to forty families. They now give a living to three. The social consequences of this new method of farming have been appalling. The effect on the *soil*, the basis of our existence, has been appalling too. Now there is just sterile dust capable of holding the crop upright while it is fed from the fertilizer bag and sprayed with poisons to keep it free enough from pests and diseases not to die. There are no four-footed animals on the farm, beyond the odd dog and cat, so there is not one ounce of 'the most valuable stuff in the world'.

I am not suggesting that farmers should *go back* to Mr Catt's type of farming. I don't believe you can ever 'go back' (although my dear but alas departed friend Fritz Schumacher once said to me: 'But when you are standing on the edge of a precipice the only sensible thing to *do* is to go back!' – And by God we are standing on the edge of a precipice now!). But modern professional organic farmers, in Europe and North America, and a few in Britain, are finding ways of *going forward* into a new way of agriculture altogether. They are the farmers of the future. There are a lot of enthusiastic amateurs: people from the cities who call themselves 'organic farmers' but have never had the humility to learn the hard long discipline of farming. They will, we hope one day, learn to become proper farmers. But where we find real professional farmers who have converted to organic farming we realize that it will be perfectly possible, one day, to feed this world's population without dousing the land with poisons and lashing on the artificial fertilizer. We will *have* to one day! For the feed stocks are running out, the oil and the gas will not last for ever, nor will the dwindling deposits of phosphate and potash. Let us do it now, before we are forced to, and before we poison and pillage our planet.

My own rules for organic husbandry are:

1  You should work with Nature and not against her;
2  Nature is diverse so you should practise diversity;
3  The two great kingdoms of Life should not be divorced from each other;
4  You should at all times strive to enrich the organic content of the soil.

Modern organic farmers do not live in the past; they are quite willing to make use of modern machinery when it suits. They are experimenting with all kinds of new techniques: trying out a huge variety of different species and breeds of plants, for example, for green manuring (growing a crop and then ploughing it in to improve the land); or for smothering weeds; or for mixed cropping. The 'agribusinessperson' has lost all contact with the traditions of the past. The modern (should we say perhaps post-modern) organic farmer respects and builds on those traditions, but is not slavishly bound by them. One little example of the blending of traditional and modern is the electric fence: this enables the farmer, without too much labour or expenditure on fencing, to *fold* animals over the land. Ancient farmers did this with sheep by *hurdling* them. I spent a winter doing this, as a boy, on the Cotswold hills. The sheep were kept on fields of turnips, behind heavy wooden hurdles, and it was my job to enclose another bite of field every day by moving these heavy hurdles forward (they seemed to weigh a ton!) and letting the animals move onto a new stretch every day. This was good for the sheep, because they did not pick up their own intestinal or pulmonary parasites (they were always on 'clean ground') and it was marvellous for the land, for the heavy dunging of the sheep, and the treading of their sharp little hooves, ensured bumper crops for the next three years.

Now, because of the electric fence, all sorts of animals can be thus 'folded' over all sorts of crops, with benefit to stock and land. Land that has been thus treated does not need 'chemicals'.

Another modern boon for the contemporary organic farmer is that he or she can keep cattle in straw yards (the very best thing to improve the *heart* of the land) without the laborious job of forking the resultant muck out with the dung-fork. A small tractor with a fore-end loader can go in and pick the stuff up and load it into a trailer, which takes it to the *mixen*, or 'muck-heap', where it should be stacked for several months to mature before it is again forked out by tractor, loaded into a tractor-drawn muck spreader, and spread on the land. I am not claiming that farmers will never go forward (you can never, by the nature of Time, 'go back') to horse-drawn equipment and hand tools again in the history of this planet. But I will state that I do not believe that they will do so as long as tractors and the fuel that drives them are available.

As for the organic farming panacea, it does not necessarily avoid the evils of over-mechanization. You can have a highly mechanized organic farm just as you can a non-organic one. Organic farming does, however, employ more *labour* per unit of crop produced, and for that reason, in a world where unemployment is a problem, should be preferred.

But how can the town or city person, who has little or nothing to do with the land, influence how the latter is treated? Well, simply by using the Power of the Purse, (which is far more powerful than the so-called 'power of the vote'). Insist on buying organic produce, whenever you can, and do so *even though*, for a time, you may have to pay a little more for it. In time the cost of organic food will be no higher than conventional produce, because, apart from any other market factors, chemicals cost a lot of money, and will cost more as the feed stocks are depleted.

It is generally conceded that organic agriculture would produce from ten to twenty per cent less food than non-organic. This would just nicely take care of the present surpluses, which are such an expensive embarrassment and which contribute so much to world food problems. Our dumping of food on hungry nations has exactly the opposite effect to that intended; it drives the local farmers out of business, for how can they grow crops to compete with *free* food? It drives the peasant from the land into the towns where the food aid is dished out. And he or she never goes back again. A French peasant said to me once: 'A peasant is like a stone on the mountainside – when the stone rolls down it never rolls up again. When a peasant rolls to the town he will never come back again.' We should strain every nerve to help the poor nations establish their traditional agriculture again and we should phase out buying their cash crops, which force the peasant off the land and only make the rich people of the cities richer. If this were done not too suddenly the countries would adjust.

We organic farmers and gardeners must prepare ourselves for a terrible backlash from the huge chemical combines. Until recently they have just looked at us as comic characters, but now they are beginning to take the organic movement seriously. We threaten their very existence. In the United Kingdom we are already beginning to see the two-page spreads in national papers showing a huge carrot on one page and a miserable little 'organic' carrot on the other. And the lies are coming: 'We could not feed the world without chemicals!' We could. 'It is animal dung and ploughed-up grassland which are nitrifying the underground water!' It isn't; it didn't in the ages of the past – why should it now? 'It is the farting of cows that is destroying the ozone layer!' Why didn't the flatulence of millions of wild buffalo, wildebeeste, buck and deer and other wild grazing animals destroy the ozone layer in the last few hundred thousand years before humans tamed cattle? Of course any stupid lie is better for the apologists for the agrochemical industry than taking any of the blame for what is going wrong with our planet. There is no doubt that we of the organic movement will, quite soon, have to meet the agrochemical industry head on. We are a direct and very serious threat to its existence. And it is an enormous industry, gigantic – a very Goliath. But look what happened to Goliath.

I would like to end this section by describing the history of the development of one particular farming operation during my own lifetime: haymaking. This story has nothing to do with 'organic' or 'non-organic', but it has everything to do with the quality of life, which is what this book is about.

When I was a boy, grass for hay (and when I say grass I mean at least as much clover as grass) was cut with the horse-drawn mower. This required either two or three strong horses to pull it and it was pretty killing work for them. The grass was then *tedded* (that is fluffed up and turned over so as to dry it) by hand with wooden rakes or pitch forks. If rain threatened it was quickly *cocked* (forked up into dome-shaped heaps that would shed the rain), and when the rain was over the cocks would be pulled to pieces so that the grass could go on drying again. This process might happen several times, and with a big field of hay this was an awful lot of labour. Finally it was considered dry enough and was cocked for the last time, maybe left a week or two and then *carried*. It was forked up onto big wagons, with someone (generally the oldest man on the farm) standing precariously on top of the load as it reached skyward. Then a rope was flung over it, the old man shinned down the rope and the wagon went off to the stackyard. There the load was forked onto a stack (which could be as big as a small cottage) and when the latter was completed, and beautifully shaped, it was thatched with straw. In the winter, when the hay was wanted, the stack was cut down vertically with a stack-knife, and very hard work that was too.

The first big change was the coming of the tractor. This pulled the mower, and as time went on tractor-drawn trailers took the place of the magnificent curved ship-like wagons. Then came the pick-up bailer and this dispensed with a great deal of labour. Farm workers were finding themselves redundant and moving to the towns. A strong man could fling a bale of hay up on to a high trailer load, and that would represent many forkfuls of loose hay. Tractor-drawn tedders took the place of rake and fork for that job. All the years I farmed in Wales we made hay like this, going round in a gang of about seven or eight neighbours all working together and making each person's hay in turn. I have no hesitation in saying that those haymaking days on the rough little farms in Pembrokeshire were the happiest days of my life. We worked hard all the long day, with the sweat pouring down us, laughing and joking and occasionally having recourse to the flagon of home-made beer, and, when darkness fell late at night we would go into the farmhouse and there would be piles of sandwiches, and home-brew drinking and singing of fine Welsh songs very often until daylight next day. The word *community* takes on a different meaning when you have had an experience like that.

But then came the Big Round Bale. This was too heavy to be lifted by men and so the hard physical labour of haymaking was over. Each farmer now worked alone, with his machines. The neighbours were not needed any more.

Parallel with changes in haymaking came a radically new method of conserving the summer flush of grass for feeding to stock in the winter: silage. If you cut green plants and enclose them from the air, carbon dioxide will be produced, expel what oxygen there is, and thereafter no decay will take place. This will produce silage. It has two great advantages for the farmer. One is that you can make it in almost any weather because you do not have to dry it, the other is that good silage has a higher protein content than indifferent hay. In addition, the whole process can be done by machine, no hand labour at all is involved.

At first the silage was made in towers, but these were expensive to build and hard to get the silage out of again. Then, with the coming of cheap plastic, it was made in heaps on the ground and covered hermetically with big sheets of black plastic. The plastic is expensive, polluting to produce, and can only be used once. Now, more and more, big bale silage is coming in; machines cut the forage, bale it in huge round bales and cover these with plastic envelopes. This process requires even more plastic than the older method did. The used plastic all has to be got rid of, and this is generally done by burning, with the inevitable production of poisonous gases. Another major drawback with silage is that it always makes more or less liquid effluent; very often this gets into the water system, and is highly toxic to aquatic life.

It is easy to see however why the practical farmer has changed from the old haymaking practices to highly mechanized silage making. But *pleasure* at work is a factor that the practical farmer, or agricultural adviser, cannot take into account. There is nothing more *boring*, and few things more unhealthy, than sitting in the cab of a tractor, with ear pads on, pulling a forage harvester up and down to make silage, or making big bale hay, where the product is never touched by human hand. One of the greatest joys in life, for a fit man or woman, is the old fashioned haymaking, where everybody works together in a happy gang, you can hear the birds sing, you feel a sense of triumph if you get your crop in unspoiled by rain (and even in wet West Wales I managed to get seventeen out of the seventeen crops of hay I got in decent condition). The sense of physical and mental well-being after a day of swinging bales up by hand, or loose hay up with pitchforks, is inestimable.

There is nothing more or less 'organic' or 'non-organic' about these different methods of conserving grass. And if we really want to have 98 per cent of our population living in cities the mechanized methods are inevitable. I just feel that a great glory has gone from the world.

# 13. Food

The other day Angela and I were given supper by a lady who was a prominent member of the local 'green' group. The meal, which we ate off plates on the formica top of a table made of some sort of reconstituted wood, consisted of 'chicken portions' fried in some rather nasty vegetable oil, potato chips fried in the same unpleasant substance, and some shrivelled peas which had been wearied to death by many years in the deep freeze. The peas had been harvested by machine long after they had passed the point of perfection, parboiled in some huge factory, frozen, and had now been dragged out of their frosty grave, boiled again (and for far too long) and dumped on our plates. There could be one reason and one reason only for eating them: and that was so as not to offend our hostess. Certainly if you fed rats on them for long enough the rats would first have got ricketts then have died from malnutrition.

I do not like to dwell on the 'chicken portions'. Suffice to say that, as I chewed on their dry and tasteless fibre, my thoughts went back constantly to the last chicken death-house I had been into. This was a deep-litter broiler house, half an acre in extent, in which thousands and thousands of dirty white wretches fought to hang on to their poor little lives for as long as possible. Some were obviously sick to the point of no return, others were dead and their brothers walked over their bodies. The stink was awful.

There were no windows, but forced ventilation, and the lights were on all the time. The animals were fed on the ground-up bodies of their predecessors. The owner had told me a supposedly harrowing tale of when the electricity supply got cut off, the ventilation fans failed, and tens of thousands of his chickens died. I thought it was a blessed release for them. The memory of this visit did not add to my enjoyment in eating the meal.

The chips were just chips, but the fact that they had been fried in that horrible factory-made oil made them taste awful. No doubt my hostess had been watching the telly advertisements of the huge international company that manufactured the stuff and therefore was convinced of its excellence. She was worried stiff about her *cholesterol* level, and that is probably why she put that greasy plastic container of margarine on the table. The fact that the stuff had been made in some huge factory hundreds of miles away, out of all kinds of substances, and that there were beautiful cows to be seen grazing not far from the kitchen window, did not seem to have occurred to this 'green' lady at all.

This kind of supper scene is not at all unusual in the industrialized world – it is the norm. British food is, by and large, *awful*. North American food, by and large, is not much better.

*The shortest road from the soil to the mouth is the best.* Green peas, picked straight from the garden at the right time of the year boiled briskly with a few leaves of mint, and eaten on a hot plate with some butter, are probably one of the greatest gastronomic experiences a person can have. If they are accompanied by new potatoes, grown with good manure and not forced on with artificials, and roast chicken, from a young cockerel that has spent a happy life running about outside – scratching for food as its wild ancestors did, ideally on your own piece of ground, or not much worse on a neighbour's – then you have a meal fit for the most deserving in the land, and you can eat it without a twinge of conscience.

This book is about *quality of life*. I submit that if there is no quality in the food that we eat then life itself has no quality and we must just hope to get through it as soon as possible. Because the source of our food has got further and further away from our tables, and the food goes through more and more industrial processing, the only quality now deemed important is a *long shelf-life*. Such food is dead food – all the life has been taken out of it. Eating irradiated food is like eating resuscitated Egyptian mummy. Food cooked in the micro-wave oven has this same dead quality. I would like to see all the microwave ovens in the world dumped onto the Atlantic Shelf, with their doors open, where they would make great homes for lobsters.

If the food we produce in our own homes is muck then we will always be searching for better, jumping in the car and going off to a restaurant where the chef comes from a foreign land where they still know about good food. We will never stay at home contentedly, we will be restless, for something inside us tells us that all is not well with the way we live. And we will get sick, sick and *tired*. We will have no *hwyl* any more – I use the Welsh word because it no longer has an English equivalent – no *joie de vivre*, no abounding energy. But above all we will be sick. Hence the sad looks and sad complexions of the people we see thronging the supermarkets of our towns – filling their trolleys with all sorts of packet rubbish.

The best source of food is our own garden – for those of

us who are lucky enough to have one; next our neighbour's. Maybe I can grow onions and they potatoes and we can swap. Next the farm down the road. Next the village shop, or the shop round the corner. But in the shop we must be sure to buy *local* food whenever we can! Exotic food – avocado pears for example, in temperate climates – is fine, as an occasional luxury, but not as staple diet. Excessive transport of goods is polluting and destroying our planet, as I have already explained.

Some time ago I happened to be in Brixham, a fishing port in South Devon. I went into a fish restaurant on the quayside and ordered some plaice. I sat, waiting for it, by the window, looking out at that ludicrous statue of William of Orange with the mandatory seagull sitting on his head – doing to him what many sensible people would have liked to have done to him while he was alive! – when a small trawler came and started unloading boxes of beautiful fat plaice onto the quayside. They looked superb.

My fish arrived – a tired and weary substance smothered in stale breadcrumbs.

'Where do you get your fish?' I asked the waitress.

'Oh it is delivered in a van. Deep frozen.'

I found the boss and asked him the same question. His answer was 'Grimsby: we get it all from Grimsby.' Grimsby is about three hundred miles from Brixham. I watched the delicious-looking plaice over the road being loaded into a huge lorry; it was going to Grimsby. *What has gone wrong with us?* What kind of sick insanity is this? What insanity is it that makes people in Kent buy 'Golden Disgusting' apples brought in huge articulated lorries from north Italy, to be eaten in the finest apple-growing country in the world, where orchards of Cox's Orange Pippin are being bulldozed because they don't pay any more? What insanity sends lorry-loads of early Pembrokeshire broccoli up to Nine Elms Market in London to be auctioned, transferred into another truck, and sent back again to be sold in the shops of Pembrokeshire? I could cite thousands of examples of such *bêtises*.

If this is all due to the 'natural workings of the market' then we must *interfere* with the natural workings of the market. We do not want to eat stale food all the time, food that has been dragged hundreds of miles from where it was grown, food that has been irradiated, sterilized, denatured, dipped in mould-inhibiting chemicals and so on and so on. I will never forget Fritz Schumacher telling me how he had been driving across America and had got out of the car to have a look at some cows. 'As I leant on the fence gazing at these magnificent animals,' he said, 'suddenly a huge tanker lorry roared past behind me. On it was written: *Pasteurized, homogenized, sterilized, long-life milk*. After the roar of it had faded away I thought I heard one of the cows murmur to her sister: "It makes me feel so *inadequate*."'

We *must* interfere with the free workings of the market if these do not agree with us. Our health and quality of life is too important to be sacrificed for any 'free workings'. Our government will not do it for us. It is all out to 'encourage trade'. It seems to *want* our native market gardeners, and fruit growers, and producers of cheese and butter and other produce to be knocked out of their home market and ruined by foreign competition. So we must take matters into our own hands. We must adamantly refuse to buy goods brought from far away if we can possibly get goods produced nearer home. There are two very strong reasons for this, both to do with the quality of life: first, fresh natural food tastes nicer and is much better for us; second, transport is very polluting. No matter how you do it, unless you go back to the sailing ship and the horse and wagon, it is polluting. The more we can do without it the better; it is poisoning our planet.

Let us consider some of our more important foodstuffs one by one.

*Bread* – the staff of life. Anyone who is likely to read this book is probably convinced that wholemeal wheaten bread is better for you than white wrapped sliced pap. The manufacturers of white bread have a great deal invested in trying to convince you otherwise. Commercial bread-factory owners (I cannot dignify them by the noble name of 'baker') *love* white flour. Why? Because white flour from hard wheat (which is generally foreign wheat) holds a great amount of air and water. (Or to be strictly accurate carbon dioxide and water). The size of the white loaf is made up chiefly by the bubbles in it (which are formed by $CO_2$), and the weight of it is made up by water. This makes it relatively cheap to produce a given quantity. That is why if you eat white bread you have to eat an enormous amount of it really to satisfy your hunger. One slice of good whole-meal bread keeps you going very much longer.

White bread was a snob thing when it was first invented, since only rich people could afford it. When poor people could get it they did, for they felt that eating white bread was more 'refined'. This attitude still exists to quite a large extent.

Children are designed by nature always to go for the things that give them the most energy with the least digestive effort. This characteristic made sense in early Stone Age times when food was scarce. But now, when starch and sugar are extremely cheap, it does not make sense. Most mothers know that they should restrain their children's craving for sweets; they should take the same attitude to white bread. People are ridiculously indulgent with their children. If you just say: 'This is the bread, it's all there is, so get used to it,' they will get used to it. And grow up to be better men and women with stronger bones and better teeth and they won't get bowel cancer. We should make our guts work *hard* – it does them good.

In cities now it is generally possible to find a good baker nearby who sells real bread. If so then we should support her or him at any cost. Bread bought in supermarkets is often chosen for its 'shelf life'. Therefore it is full of additives. If there is no good local supply of real bread then I strongly urge people to bake their own. This is far easier than you might suppose. Done by the most sensible method it entails five minutes in the evening just before you go to bed (when you dump some flour in a bowl and stir some warm water, sugar and yeast into it) and maybe half an hour before breakfast the next day. Good whole meal bread will keep well for a week so you don't have to bake often. Some people freeze bread so one baking a month, say, will keep them supplied. (The author's *The Complete Book of Self Sufficiency* [Corgi] gives a tried recipe).

To end this dissertation on bread I would like to quote from the writings of a woman who no doubt knew far more about it than I. This is a passage from *The American Woman's Home* – a book published quite soon after the American Revolution:

Some persons prepare bread for the oven by simply mixing it in the mass, without kneading, pouring it into pans, and suffering it to rise there. The air-cells in bread thus prepared are coarse and uneven; the bread is as inferior in delicacy and nicety to that which is well kneaded as a raw servant to a perfectly educated and refined lady. The process of kneading seems to impart an evenness to the minute air cells, a fineness of texture, and a tenderness and pliability to the whole substance, that can be gained in no other way.

In other words: heed not the siren song of the no-kneaders.

*Dairy Produce*    Having made cheese, off and on, for thirty years, I am in a position to talk about it. Like other foodstuffs and beverages which have been formed from a raw material by natural processes, such as action by yeasts or bacteria, cheese was probably discovered by accident.

If you leave milk for quite a short time in a warm climate it will go sour. This is chiefly due to bacteria, mainly *Bacillus lacticus*. In souring the milk separates out into curds and whey: the familiar 'junket' of the nursery and Little Miss Muffett. If you drain the whey off the curds and just leave the latter alone they will turn into soft cheese. As by that time many other organisms besides *B.lacticus* will have invaded it, it probably won't taste very nice.

How *rennet* was discovered will probably always be a mystery. But some genius who was of far greater benefit to humankind than the man who invented the internal combustion engine found that if you dropped some of the lining of one of a calf's four stomachs into fresh milk it curdled it immediately. This cut out the long time it would have taken to have curdled naturally, and thus shortened the time available for alien micro-organisms to invade. It was also discovered that if you hang curds and whey up in a bag made of porous cloth the consequent draining of it made better cheese. Soft cheese, or cottage cheese, is still made in just this way. Curdle milk by dropping some rennet in it, hang the curds in a cheese-cloth bag for a day or two, and you will have cottage cheese.

Then some other genius (probably a woman because most of the really *useful* inventions have been made by people of that sex – she was of far more benefit to humankind than the foolish fellow who invented the firearm) found that if you applied pressure to the curds they would coalesce into a hard substance which would keep for months and even years. Thus hard cheese was invented, one of the greatest boons of the human race, since it enables us to store the summer flush of milk for the winter time.

Refinements were made down through the ages until cheese-making reached its peak probably about sixty or seventy years ago. Cheese was made on the farm, mostly by the women, and the cheese of every farm had a subtly different flavour from that of the others, because of variations in the infinitely complex bacterial and fungal mix that caused maturation. The best cheddars of my childhood were noble and magnificent, particularly when they were a year or two old.

Happy accidents occurred. A shepherd in the Roquefort area of France had the habit of leaving his daily snack of bread and cheese in a cave. One day he left it there for several days (could he have been chased away by a wolf?) and returned to find that it was blue and tasted absolutely delicious. Whether he tried to keep his secret and had to have it dragged out of him by torture, or whether he joyfully acclaimed it to the world, we will never know, but at any rate hundreds of tonnes of what many people think is the best cheese in the world are being matured right now in that huge limestone cave in the hills above Roquefort. A certain inn in the village of Stilton, in Huntingdonshire, used to serve a semi-soft (non-pressed) blue cheese made by certain local farmers' wives who happened to have the right mix of moulds in their dairies. Travellers who were riding up and down the Great North Road discovered this cheese, and the fame of 'stilton' spread throughout the land. The stiltons of my childhood were lovingly wrapped in clean white napkins, and sometimes fed with port before Christmas, and were delicious beyond any telling of it. But alas, one thinks twice before helping oneself to stilton from the cheese-boards of today. It can be deadly dull.

The reason for this is that most stiltons today are made from pasteurized milk in huge factories. There *are* still farmhouse makers of stilton in the land today, and if you are lucky enough to get a cheese from one of them you may be rewarded with the *real* flavour of stilton, but once you start making cheese in factory conditions you must inevitably compromise.

Farmhouse cheese is made from last night's milk mixed with this morning's. It just happens that this is, and always has been and always will be, the best way to do it. But a big factory cannot arrange this. So milk is kept chilled in bulk tanks, brought together in huge tanker lorries to the factory (it will inevitably be from a number of milkings) and pasteurized. The pasteurization kills all the natural bacteria in the milk and so cultured bacteria are introduced instead. This culture works reliably and consistently but cannot have the subtlety and complexity of a naturally-occurring bacterial and fungal mix of a clean, well-aired, dairy. The cheese that comes out of the factory is edible, but characterless.

There is a disease rife among large modern dairy herds (which you practically never see in small hand-milked herds) called mastitis. I don't believe a single large commercial herd is free from it. It is partially controlled by squirting penicillin or streptomycin or other antibiotic up the teats of the affected animals. In *theory* milk from such treated cows should not be put into the bulk tank for at least forty-eight hours after injection. In *practice* it very often is. A man with a hundred and fifty cows to milk twice a day does not have time for niceties and you can't have an inspector on every farm. And the antibiotic plays havoc with the benevolent bacteria needed for cheese-making. The big cheese factory just cannot avoid this problem. A farmer producing his or her own milk to make farm cheese will care for the herd lovingly, and it will probably not have very much mastitis, if any. (The cows will also be fed on the right food – which is very important.)

In Holland I was taken over the biggest cheese factory in the world. Tanker lorries were queueing up at the milk intake all day, pumping in thousands of gallons of milk from a hundred different farms, over which it would be impossible to have any sort of quality control. The milk flowed into huge pools inside, each one big enough to make an Olympic swimming pool. Eight bored unskilled labourers, a couple of chemists and the manager made up the entire workforce. The whey was dried and shipped off to America to form the basis for those disgusting *pizzas* so beloved of the inhabitants. The cheese itself, totally 'untouched by human hand' can only be sold to the English. The Dutch, who have a fine palate for cheese, will not eat it. Not one cheese from that factory is sold in Holland, or in France. The Dutch nation eat only their fine farm-made cheese: either *nieuw kaas*, young cheese, or *oud kaas* which can be a couple of years old; both are superb.

I tasted two samples of the cheese made in the-biggest-cheese-factory-in-the-world and both were characterless and tasteless. One was three months old and the other over a year. There was absolutely no pleasure whatever to be had from eating either of them.

Most of us who are old enough to have experienced the advent into Britain of the magnificent French soft and semi-soft cheeses – the bries and camemberts and pont l'eveques – after the Second World War, have noticed the great falling-off in flavour of the majority of them. It is *not* just that our palates are becoming jaded, because when we *do* get a sample of the real farm-produced semi-soft, either from France or from our own country, we re-live the fine old experience. The reason is that more and more of these traditional farmhouse cheeses of the French peasant are being made in factories.

So how can we change our lifestyles in respect to cheese? Well fortunately there are more and more enthusiasts setting up as farm cheese-makers in these British Islands, and in the Republic of Ireland too, and there is just beginning to be a revival of farm cheese-making in France. It may take a new cheese-maker a few years to perfect the art. After all making fine cheese is an art. It can never be reduced to a science, which is why a factory can never achieve the subtle quality that a farm cheese-maker can. Good cheese is the result of tender loving care.

We should *seek out* cheese, new or mature, hard or semi-soft or soft, made *on the farm* by dedicated cheese-makers who use the milk from their own cows, goats or sheep, thus controlling the whole process from the grass in the fields to the final maturing in the store. We should discriminate even among them and seek out the products which are most pleasing to us. We should insist on tasting cheese in the shop before we buy it, and asking who made it and where it came from. We should be willing, if necessary, to pay a few pennies more for the more satisfying product. We should wield the power of the purse.

And do not let us be fobbed off by the machinations of the big industrial cheese manufacturers. They will try to discredit the farm cheese-maker by every means they can. I know of one farm cheesery in Ireland, making magnificent cheese, which was closed down after a microscopic examination of a dozen samples of cheese was alleged to have discovered some listeria bacteria. Not one *case* of listeria could in fact be shown to have been caused by eating this cheese (I've been eating it for years and am still in rude health). If you search far enough in any organic product you will find a whole zoo, or Kew Gardens, of bacteria: if you search long enough you are bound to find examples of nearly anything. The listeria epidemic in England, now fortunately long forgotten, was *not* caused by people eating cheese, whether pasteurized or non-pasteurized.

Pasteurization and sterilization are methods for mummifying milk – giving it 'a longer shelf life'. The only disease we need worry about, bovine tuberculosis, was eliminated in Great Britain and North America decades ago. Good natural fresh milk, and the products made from it, should be part of the birthright of every human being, for in it lies health, and positive health too, not just absence of disease. If health 'experts' tell you otherwise take no notice of them.

*Meat*    Great controversy rages over this and this author does not intend to enter into it. All I know is that humans have been omnivorous throughout history. Paleolithic

Man painted animal-hunting scenes on the walls of his caves, not cabbages. *Homo habilis* ate meat and so did *Ramapithecus*. And as an organic farmer I would have found it very difficult to have kept up the fertility of my land except with the dung of animals. I do not think we have a right to divorce the animal kingdom from the vegetable one: the two have been interlocked since nearly the beginning of Life on this planet. And we cannot have animals without either having predators to control their numbers or else doing it ourselves.

It is commonly held by people who cannot accept that humans should kill animals (although it is apparently all right for lions) that it should be possible to keep farm animals without killing any. Such people have simply not thought the matter through. A hen will lay eggs and we could, if we were rich enough, go on feeding her until she dies of old age, but for every hen hatched in the world there is a little cock. A few minutes with a pocket calculator will show you that if we did not kill any cockerels, and if there were no predators, we would so populate the farm with cockerels that there would be room for nothing else. A cow will give us milk and again we could keep her until she dies of old age – but she will not give us milk unless she has a calf every year and every other calf is going to be a little bull. Now a very small proportion of her female calves might be kept, or sold, for replacements to the milking herd but what are we going to do with all those bulls? Each one might well drag on for thirty years and unless you have kept cattle you can have no idea how much it costs to feed one.

Having said all this I can perfectly sympathize with people who will not eat meat because they object to the outrageous manner in which many farm animals are treated nowadays. It is only because few people have seen the inside of a 'factory farm' building that any meat produced in such places can be sold at all.

But it is *not* necessary to keep animals like that. And it is perfectly possible, nowadays, to obtain meat, eggs and milk that have been produced humanely. We should insist on doing so. They cost a bit more? Then pay the bit more and do without that extra hi-fi stack or new satellite television aerial. If I couldn't obtain humanely produced meat I would not eat meat at all.

*Fruit and Vegetables*     There is only one thing to be said about these and that is, get them from as near your home as possible. If you insist on local produce then shops will begin to stock it. Every shopper buying fruit or vegetables should ask the shopkeeper *where does it come from*? If they don't know then don't buy it. If it comes from abroad the answer should be the same. They will soon get the message.

*Apples*     The apple should be to the English what the grape is to the French: an object of affection, veneration and pride. For England *was* the premier apple growing country of the world. In the National Apple Register, kept at the Royal Horticultural Society gardens at Wisley, there are the names of 4,212 varieties of apples! Most of these were developed in England: not Scotland, Ireland or Wales, but England. Now many of these varieties of apple grown on organically rich soil, in what is the proper part of the country to suit them, allowed to ripen naturally on the tree, picked carefully and stored in the right conditions (at the correct temperature and humidity) and eaten at their perfection, will provide a really great gastronomic experience. The difference between this experience and that of eating a shop-bought Golden Delicious, which probably had fifteen different poison sprays squirted on it during its period of growth in far away North Italy, had a hormone spray to make it stick to its tree long after it should naturally have been picked, an 'abscission' spray later to allow it to be picked easily and then was stored in a gas store to prevent it going rotten before being sold, and was sold after being carted right across Europe in a huge lorry; the difference between these two experiences is immense.

The Euro-apple, as the Golden Delicious has become, is not so altogether horrible as to earn the title given it by many people of 'Golden Disgusting'. It is *just passable*. You must wash it very carefully before eating it of course, and to be really safe you should peel it too. Even this will not save you from consuming some traces of biocides, for it will have been sprayed with systemic insecticides – and these get right into every cell of the plant, including the fruit. The flavour, if you are lucky enough to get a good one, can be described as ... mediocre. Certainly not 'delicious'. But also not disgusting. Yet if you are lucky enough to get, say, a Gravenstein (actually originally a German apple) or a Laxton Superb, or a Cox, or a James Grieve, organically grown and at its peak of perfection, then you will realize that you are having an experience of another order altogether. But I have seen the horrible sight, in Kent as in other English counties, of acres and acres of fine English apple trees being grubbed out, for it has been laid down by the pundits of Brussels and Luxembourg that Europe's apples shall be of one variety only, Golden Delicious, and that they shall all be grown either in the South of France or in Northern Italy. I have stood on a hillside in the South Tyrol and looked at a hundred acres of Golden Delicious trees, and heard the owner tell me, proudly, that he could control the *size* of these apples with complete accuracy, merely by measuring the dose of nitrogen he gave to each tree, and closely monitoring also the water. The Germans liked a slightly larger apple than the English. He could satisfy both tastes. He could produce a crop of apples of an exactly uniform size. There would not be one blemish on any apple because of the huge range of poisonous sprays he used. They would be perfect. But, as far as a real apple connoisseur is concerned, perfectly useless. They could not even be fed safely to pigs.

Such now is the state of the palate of European city people that most of them would be perfectly willing to eat a turnip, believing it was an apple, provided that enough money had been spent on advertising to persuade them that an apple is what it was.

So what are we to do if we decide that what we want is *real apples*? Well of course, if we have enough land, we can grow our own. True, it will be three or four years before we can get many, if we have to plant trees from scratch. True, we must have quite a lot of land if we want to grow a serious quantity of apples. A mature standard apple tree, say ten years old, may give us a hundred or two fine apples, maybe even more, but it will probably need one other variety of apple to pollinate it, and the two may well take up three hundred square feet of ground.

You can, however, get quite a good yield of apples from a smaller area of ground if you grow espalier trees, or cordons, or other closely pruned and trained tree forms on dwarfing root stocks. This is not the book in which to convey complete instructions about apple growing (the reader might consult the same author's *The Self Sufficient*

*Gardener*) but it is worth suggesting the idea of planting apples to people who have gardens. Find a worthy nurseryman and ask him what varieties of apple are likely to do best in your particular soil. An apple tree could be with you for a very long time so you might as well take some trouble to get the right one. Find out about its keeping qualities and be careful about varieties that need other varieties as pollinators.

But what of the person who has no garden, or one who feels that no space can be spared for apple trees? Is she or he condemned to a lifetime of nothing but Golden-whatever-you-like-to-call-'ems or perhaps, occasionally when lucky, some English-grown Cox's Orange Pippins – out of the gas store, chemical residues and all – or perhaps some Worcester Pearmains, probably grown on the wrong soil (i.e. not Old Red Sandstone), or even worse?

Well no. There is hope, if only at present a glimmer. There are in this world organic orchardists who grow good sound chemical-free apples and store them properly before marketing them. If you can find such a person why not visit him or her during the picking season and buy a quantity of apples to take home and store? Storing apples is quite straight forward. They should not touch each other. Temperature should be pretty low: say from −2 to 3°C (30 to 35°F). Humidity, though, should be pretty high, otherwise they shrivel. An earthen-floored stone or concrete shed will probably be damp and cool enough. 80 to 95 per cent humidity is about right. You can buy a hygrometer that measures it. Our ancestors used their judgement and common sense and had fine apples. If you wish to ripen a batch of apples quickly and to perfection put them in a higher temperature – and with a higher humidity. Then they will quickly ripen but thereafter not keep so long.

English apples, if you buy keepers, should last until March and maybe even longer. Early varieties are good in September (some, like Beauty of Bath, even in August) so this gives you seven months of happy apple-eating: the very peak and perfection of it. In the summer there is of course a surfeit of soft fruit, with plums and cherries coming in to take over to bide us through until apples come again. If we are so spoilt that we must have apples in July, and strawberries in December, then we deserve what we get: mediocre rubbish.

So, the advice to the searcher for *real* fruit is: urge our greengrocers to supply English apples if we live in England, organically grown apples whether we live in England or not (don't jib if the apples supplied are not all of exactly the same size – or if some of them even have a harmless blemish or two: a slightly discoloured apple will do us far more good than one that has been sprayed with poison); and encourage him to experiment with varieties. Experiment ourselves with varieties and different storing periods. Discover again the great range and magnificent subtle qualities of that great heritage: the English apple.

*Grains and pulses*    It is quite wrong to buy large amounts of these from Third World countries. By doing so you are starving the poor people there, and putting money into the pockets of the rich people who do the exporting. So-called 'greenies' who live on soya bean and other products from the Third World just haven't thought the thing through. They are not being 'green' at all. They are encouraging the very forces that are destroying our planet. People who emigrate to other climate-zones should learn to eat the foods produced there.

*

*Fish* This is the finest and most healthful of high-protein food for humans and it should be possible for us all to eat plenty of it. *But* somehow we have got to conserve the wild fish stocks, otherwise we shall end up without any fish to eat. The present huge investment by the industrial countries in enormous fishing vessels, with ever more murderous gear, is devastating the wild fish stocks. We have to tackle this problem before it is too late. The present free-for-all is a perfect example of the Tragedy of the Commons. The first thing to do would be to give every country the control over its own sea areas, then at least conservation might begin. The Icelanders won not only a great battle for their fishermen, but also for the *fish*, when they secured a hundred mile limit around their coasts. All other maritime nations should do the same.

The policy of the European Community on sea fishing has been absolutely disastrous. In order to 'keep the price up', fish that don't make a certain price in the fish auctions are 'bought into intervention'. They are then sprayed with dye and the fishermen are paid to take them out to sea and dump them. Fishermen, in some cases, are given 'quotas'. Mackerel fishermen for example are only allowed to land a certain quantity of fish. So huge ring-netters go to sea, encircle hundreds of tonnes of fish – which are all killed as the net is hauled in close – take just the quota allowed on board, and then dump the rest to rot at the bottom of the sea. These practices are the result of allowing politicians and accountants, and so-called 'scientists', to dictate policies on subjects about which they know nothing. *Ask the people who fish* – they really *do* know.

A word must be said about *fish farming*. Some of us hoped that the development of this would help to save the wild stocks. There is no reason why it shouldn't. But, entirely because of the snob appeal of so-called *game fish* – i.e. salmon and trout – fish farmers have concentrated on these. The fact that farmed salmon and trout are not worth eating does not seem to matter: people will still order them in restaurants because of their aura of having been, for many years, the food of the wealthy. Salmon and trout are carnivorous fish, and therefore the least suitable for fish farming for two main reasons. The first is that wild fish stocks are ruthlessly destroyed to provide the food for farmed fish. What is the sense of catching wild fish – which would be delicious to eat themselves – and grinding them up and feeding them to tame fish? The other is that fish fed on other fish are more polluting and the huge quantity of excreta from salmon cages is grossly polluting the environment.

It would be far better to farm herbivorous fish, such as members of the Carp family, or Tilapia, or Catfish, or many others. We could thus turn low-grade vegetable matter into first-class protein and we would not be depleting the wild fish stocks at all.

# THE FUTURE OF CHANGE

# 14. Where We Are Now

Throughout this book my contention has been that if we make the necessary changes voluntarily, and *soon enough*, we can immeasurably *improve* the quality of our lives. We will have to alter though our perception of what we really want – what we really need. We will have to learn the difference between true civilization and the kind of materialistic barbarism that passes for 'civilization' in much of the Western world today. We will have to replace the reign of quantity with a new reign of quality in our hearts and in our lives.

To make radical change will not be easy you say? No: nothing that is really worthwhile is ever easy. But the quality of the lives of the people who are to follow after us – of our children and our childrens' children – will depend entirely on whether or not we are able to make the right changes now.

If we look back over human history we will assure ourselves that there have been drastic changes in lifestyle at practically every stage. Since *Ramapithecus* emerged from the trees, some twenty million years ago, and found it convenient to walk upright instead of on all fours, we have been making drastic changes. Probably *Ramapithecus* didn't make this change because she wanted to but because she *had* to. Perhaps she didn't so much leave the forest as the forest left her, for changing climate in that part of the world disfavoured trees. Perhaps it was necessary to stand upright to see over the tall grasses, instead of crouch down to see under the trees. (It is this evolutionary trait which explains why the horse, a grassland animal, always gets up from a lying position front-end first, while the ox, a forest creature, gets up rear-end first.) I have no doubt that the individuals who made this radical change in lifestyle tended to survive while the ones who refused to change did not.

When creatures of our own species, people of the New Stone Age, discovered, ten thousand years ago, that you can plant edible grass seeds and harvest a crop, and agriculture began there was another very radical change of lifestyle. This discovery led to the first human settlement – for the hunter-gatherer cannot settle in one place whereas the farmer must. And, as I have already explained, it led to the complete destruction of the soil of that first-ever cultivated country.

There have been hundreds of other very radical changes in the lifestyles of our ancestors. If you had told an informed English person in 1750 that before a hundred years had passed most English people would be living in cities they would never have believed you. Yet by 1850 most of them were. Nowadays the true country person is a pretty rare bird. And who knows what will be happening in a hundred years from now? There is only one thing we can predict about the future, and that is that it will be quite unlike what any of us predict. Absolutely no one – no one anywhere on either side of the Iron Curtain – would have predicted, in October 1989, that within a month people would begin to pull down the Berlin Wall. There are going to have to be dramatic changes in lifestyle due to that.

And so it behoves us to be prepared to change our lifestyles drastically at any time, and to do it voluntarily, and quickly, and not to wait until events overtake us. The

Ramapithecines who refused to make the change to walking upright became extinct: the ones who made that change survived and are almost certainly our ancestors.

When we look to the future we have three basic choices: we can continue as we are at present, short-sightedly guzzling finite resources in a crazy rush of consumerism; we can attempt to mollify some of the grosser aspects of consumerism and try still to hang on to our present 'living standards'; or we can change, willingly, profoundly and radically. In the last three chapters of this book I will look at each of these scenarios.

# 15. The Continued Growth Scenario

In this scenario the world goes on much as it is going now, only more so. Most politicians – or at least the ones that are in power in the world – most businessmen, most bankers and financiers, think that this is the way the world will go on. After all, ever since the invention of the steam engine industrial growth has continued, in an ever steepening curve, and why should it stop now? The British Chancellor of the Exchequer said the other day that there was only one way to stop inflation, and that was by having more and more *growth*, by which he meant of course industrial growth, not the growth of virtue or of the human spirit.

And, the way things are, he is probably right. We are constantly told that we must have 3 or 4 per cent *growth* per annum to prevent an increase in unemployment. And we have got to compete haven't we? We have got to compete against simply everybody in the world. If we cannot produce motor cars as cheaply as the Japanese can then Japanese motor cars will flood into this country and put an end to the native industry and thousands of people will lose their jobs. But you can only produce motor cars, and all other mass-produced goods, cheaply if you do it on a huge scale. Therefore we must enlarge our motor car industry; and so must every other car-producing country in the world.

We must constantly crank up our 'industrial efficiency',

strive for greater and greater industrial output. We must turn our education system over more and more to industry-related subjects. This means, inevitably, neglecting more and more the humanities, the subjects that train the brain to enjoy high quality of living, the good things of life. We must be prepared to reward the successful even more highly and let the people who do not want this competitive, aggressive, lifestyle sink to the scrap heap, where they belong.

Of course in one sense the business people and their like are quite right; if industrial growth ceased in any country then that country, too, would fall to the world equivalent of the scrap heap. If industrial growth ceased in any classical industrial society there would be massive unemployment, and unrest. If growth ceased there would be a stock market crash: shares would tumble, millions would go bankrupt. Karl Marx, who was seldom right, was right in his analysis of the fundamental flaw in capitalism; he believed that the only way capitalist nations could resolve this problem was by pouring their surplus industrial production into useless projects: which meant, almost inevitably, war.

Marx realized that the capitalist market could not absorb the production of capitalist industry because, inevitably, money got into too few hands. A millionaire can only sleep in one bed, drive about in one car at a time and so on, so that surplus wealth doesn't get spent and the millionaire has to invest it in yet *more* industry.

Modern business people are very aware of this contradiction. How are they going to *sell* the vast output from their constantly expanding industries? Well they have to use the advertising industry of course. How else can they persuade their customers to consume more and more and more? 'We *must* get people out of this silly habit of owning only one car per family. How else can our car industry sell its ever-increasing product?' 'We *must* persuade people to have a television in every room.' Including the jakes. I know a man who has two in his living room – so that wherever he sits he does not have to turn his head to look at 'Neighbours'. Growth must go on for ever and ever and ever of course – as long as the world lasts.

There is not only the home market, there are all those foreigners too. They must be persuaded to take our industrial production at all costs. If they cannot afford to buy our produce then we must lend them the money so they can. And if they cannot afford to pay the loans back again – or to 'service' them at an ever-increasing rate of interest – then we must lend them *more* money so they can. And even *more* money, so they can build up an industrial economy to generate the funds to pay us back what they owe us. But there is a slight contradiction here which has escaped our learned economists. If they do build up such an industrial base then they won't be needing the products of our industry any more will they? And what will happen then to our *growth*?

To go on for ever lending people money to pay the interest on money we have already lent them – and then lending them more money to pay the interest on the last lot of money, may seem a questionable economy. My bank manager will not do it with me – what have the Brazilians and Argentinians got that I have not?

But all this is called 'rescheduling debts' and it is all part of the Growth Economy don't you see? And remember we are in direct competiton with every other industrially developed nation in the world about this. They are all scrambling to lend money and dump goods. So we cannot be too fussy about whom we lend to – we've got to get in first.

The effect of these global economic policies on the Third World is absolutely disastrous. Their rich get richer and their poor get poorer, until the latter are absolutely destitute. The land on which the poor have been growing crops to feed themselves is taken away by the rich to grow cash crops to sell to the West to get more money to spend on luxury goods.

Nairobi was a large village when I knew it fifty years ago; now it is a city of sky scrapers, (surrounded by slums of course). There is an enormous round monstrosity in the middle which I was told was the biggest conference centre in the world. Now, a country sliding fast into desertification and famine needs the biggest conference centre in the world like it needs an atomic explosion. People talk all the time of the new tribe that has risen up in East Africa. In addition to the Wakamba and the Watende and the Waswahili they now have the Wabenzi; to be a member of this you have to own a Mercedes Benz. Over-population and over-stocking, owing to people having been driven off their ancestral land so that the Wabenzi can grow such things as pineapples and cut flowers to sell to the industrial nations, are destroying the countryside. Deforestation, mostly caused by the demand for charcoal to cook the food of the million people who live in Nairobi, leads to yet more soil destruction.

In Europe in 1989 a vast new factor came into play with the breaking down of the Iron Curtain. Almost unimaginably large markets have suddenly opened up to the West. And the trade that these will give rise to will not be the same kind of trade as the West has with the Third World, for the Eastern Bloc countries will quickly develop their own industry. Only for a short time will they require our consumer goods. Then they will be competing in our own markets against our own industry. They will whole-heartedly join in the West's economy of *growth* and the industrial production of the world could well quadruple in a decade or two. This will spell even greater disaster for the Third World.

But it is not to be. The continued growth scenario cannot actually come about. Let us consider one item of industrial output only: the motor car.

There are roughly 667 million inhabitants of what might be called the car-owning countries now, and there are 4,276 million in the substantially non car-owning ones. We know about the Wabenzi of course, and their equivalents elsewhere, but by and large Third World and the Eastern Bloc countries are not car-owning countries. In 1986 the World Watch Institute in Washington D.C. predicted that at the present rate of oil consumption, and putting the estimate for yet undiscovered sources of petroleum at the level of the highest guess: 'The ultimate depletion of global oil resources is between 50 and 88 years away.' But imagine if there were *six times* the number of cars in the world? It is obvious that before most of those extra cars are actually manufactured there will be no oil to run them on. Furthermore, the atmosphere of this planet has already been chemically altered to a dangerous degree by the motor cars we have already got. What will happen to the atmosphere if the cars are multiplied by six?

Electric cars, you may say, may replace petrol and diesel ones. But where is the increased electrical power to come from? Even the thousand new power stations that China hopes to build in the next decade will be nothing like enough to charge the batteries of all the electric cars that the Chinese will have to build to bring themselves up to, say, the current level of car ownership in the United States. To do this they would need to build, or buy, more than five hundred million electric cars. And although research into battery storage has been going on since the last century, no great breakthrough has yet been achieved: batteries are still expensive, heavy, and highly polluting. And as for the plethora of power stations that would be needed to charge all these batteries – what will they do to the greenhouse effect and the ozone layer?

Cars of course are only one example (although an important one) of the assault that the policy of unre-strained growth-for-ever is having on our planet. It must be obvious to any business person who can lift his or her eyes from the profit and loss account for more than a few minutes that this policy is unsustainable.

# 16. The Palliative Scenario

In this we go on more or less as we are going, but try to take palliative measures to reduce the malign impact of what we are doing.

Taking lead out of petrol was one palliative measure, and a very good thing too: it should never have been put there in the first place. Fitting efficient filters on power station chimneys is another. Trying (no matter how half-heartedly) to develop renewable sources of energy: solar, wind, water, tide, thermal, biomass and biogas, thus reducing our dependance on fossil fuel or nuclear fuel, is another. And then there is recycling, which a few people are beginning to take seriously. All these things are good in themselves, but I am afraid they are just not going to prove enough.

You can take most of the sulphur out of coal or oil smoke for example, thus reducing acid rain damage, but it is almost impossible to stop carbon dioxide emissions; if you burn hydrocarbon fuel you generate $CO_2$, and that is that. The same thing applies to catalytic converters in car exhausts. They get some of the nasties out: nitrogen oxide, carbon-monoxide and various hydro-carbons are made to react together by the platinum catalyst within the exhaust system, but they do not solve the big problem caused inevitably by burning fossil fuel – they do not reduce the $CO_2$ emission. In fact they slightly increase it.

There are prices to pay too. Scrubbers in power station

chimneys require huge quantities of limestone to make them work. This entails massive quarrying operations: more hillsides being blasted open and destroyed. The disposal of the huge amount of sulphurous waste is another severe problem. A fraction of it can be taken up by the building industry but most of it will have to be dumped one way or another.

Such things are palliatives, but palliatives is all they will ever be. *You cannot solve the problems created by technology by more technology.*

I saw one illustration of this principle when I went to a small lake called Baldegger See in Switzerland. As I have explained (p. 134), technology has made it possible to keep *pigs* in great concentrations, crammed into intensive housing. Thus around the Baldegger See, as around many another lake in Europe there are intensive pig units. But many pigs together produce much slurry, not to give it a plainer name. Slurry never goes uphill; it always goes down. There is so much of it that the land cannot absorb it. Therefore it inevitably ends in the ditches, the streams, and eventually the lake. In the lake it deprives the fish of oxygen and they die.

I went to the Baldegger See with a BBC camera crew: we were making some films about the environment. We went there because *more technology* has been called in to repair the damage that technology has caused; they were pumping oxygen through the water. The oxygen was carried from a factory far away, in huge tanker lorries, being pumped into static tanks on the lake side and from there led to perforated pipes on the lake bottom.

The cost of this was astronomical. Lanes were having to be widened to get the tankers there. Many other lakes in Switzerland were to be treated in the same way, so more tanker lorries would have to be applied, another factory built to create the oxygen, more lanes widened, more little villages polluted with heavy traffic, more acid rain damage caused to the already dying trees of the Alps, more damage done to the atmosphere and the ozone layer.

The engineer in charge asked me what I thought about the scheme; wasn't it fine, soon fish would be able to live in that lake again! I told him that I thought it was the silliest thing I had ever seen.

'Remove the *cause*,' I said.

'But that is political – I am an engineer,' he said.

The palliative method can be seen very clearly in our solutions to traffic problems. More and more of our dwindling countryside is to be put under tarmac; more and more of our frightfully valuable city space is going under car parks (and you can still never find anywhere to park). More and more property is being destroyed to make room for urban freeways, or underpasses, or overpasses or other devices to speed the flow of traffic, a bigger and bigger army is being employed in clamping vehicles, or towing cars away, or fining motorists; and yet the congestion problem in our cities gets worse and worse.

The supporters of the palliative scenario say: 'Build *more* underpasses, or overpasses, knock more houses down to make more city freeways, by-pass the by-passes and by-pass the by-passes of the by-passes and we will win in the end.' But we will not.

It is very hard for we who are at present depending on motoring not to give a secret cheer when traffic jams are relieved by improvements to a congested motorway or other highway. Generally, after a very few months, the cheer is converted into a groan as we learn yet again that *roads generate traffic:* the traffic problem gets worse, not better. *The only solution to the traffic problem is less traffic.*

But this would mean less trade? Yes, it would mean less trade! there is far too much trade. Biscuits, baked in Dundee, are hauled all the way south to be sold in Reading. Biscuits baked in Reading are hauled all the way up to Dundee. The lorries carrying them pass each other on the M1 and, having delivered their loads, go back empty.

Proponents of the continued growth scenario would ask what is wrong with that? After all, building the lorries, transporting the oil, maintaining the roads all make employment and, also, they generate money. And the people who make the money pay taxes which help pay the dole of the people who do not have jobs. Also, we are free people, why should we not have choice? Maybe there are people in Dundee who *like* Reading biscuits. Maybe there are people in Reading who don't.

My position is that we cannot afford to be so choosy. Transport – particularly road transport – is extremely polluting, just about the most polluting thing there is. I am not saying that we should have no trade, I am saying that we should have far *less* trade. There would not be less employment if biscuits had to be made locally and not transported vast distances from huge factories, there would be more. The employment lost to the transport industry would be more than made up for by the increased number of people a large number of small factories would employ. The free workings of the market, coupled with transport so cheap as to be almost not worth taking into account, have led to a vast volume of long-distance transport which is totally unnecessary. Is it really necessary, or desirable, to drink Australian beer in England, or indeed Danish beer? Britain can brew perfectly good beer of its own. Is it really necessary to haul Newcastle Brown Ale to Cornwall. The people of Cornwall could perfectly well learn to drink good Cornish beer. Trade, particularly road-borne trade, has gone mad. The pollution it is causing, the destruction of our cities and countryside, is catastrophic.

No, the only way to solve the traffic problem is to have less traffic. It will have to happen one day whatever we do or don't do. It will either happen by a backlash of Nature – the oil getting scarcer and more expensive, or the atmosphere getting so polluted that even our politicians will notice it – or it will happen because we decide to *make* it happen. Because we realize the desperate seriousness of the situation we are getting into.

One of the great shibboleths of the palliative scenario lobby is that we need more industry to generate the money to pay for repairing the damage already caused by industry. But we cannot mitigate the damage caused by industry by creating more; we can only do it by having less.

That again will put people out of work? It is my contention that it will create *more* work. For less big industry will mean more small industry, which employs more labour. Establishing tree nurseries and planting forests takes labour, not money. Better insulation of houses takes a little money but a lot of labour. Construction of renewable energy devices is labour intensive not capital intensive. As I have already said, it costs hundreds of thousands of pounds to establish one work place in a huge automated factory: a couple of thousand will set a man up as a carpenter or a shoemaker. Putting money into highly mechanized and highly robotized jobs is a rotten way to provide employment: you get very few jobs for your money.

We will save our planet by spending less money, not more money. Paradoxically we will provide more employment by spending less money too.

No, the palliative scenario will not work. It will not save our planet. Technology is not going to cure the ills that technology has caused. Only a fundamental change in our whole attitude to the world, to life, to work, and to consumption can do that.

# 17. The Radical Change Scenario

This is the only one that has any chance of saving our world.

There was a popular song about when I was a boy the refrain of which went: The best things in life are free!

Well they are, or nearly so. It is because we have forgotten this that we have got our world into such a muddle. What does a sensible woman or man really need to be happy? Health, of course, and health – real positive health not just absence of disease – can only be got by hard manual work or exercise, fresh air, sunshine, secure shelter and unadulterated food. All but the last two items of this list are free.

Love. After health love is essential to the good life and is I have always been given to understand, free.

A house, warm and dry and beautiful. Considering the inflated price of housing in most western countries nowadays it may come as a shock to realize that housing could be free too. If houses were built to last (which alas they are not) and if the population were stable (which alas it isn't) housing would be free to most of us as it passed from old to new generations. The population will have to stabilize one day, whether we like it or not, or there will be standing room only on this planet and then half of us will have to sit on the other half's shoulders.

Fun and conviviality. This still exists, in spite of the television, and it is free too. And if we need beer, to lubricate it, we can brew this ourselves and even if we have to buy the malt and the hops these cost a few pennies not shillings. And after all – wine is only 'the fruit of the vine and the work of human hands' and these things are the gifts of God and should be free.

For literate people there is literature. This can, in civilized countries, be free if there are public libraries. And the making of books does not impose a heavy tax on our planet. The acreage of trees cut down to make books is negligible compared to that needed for newspapers and a book may last centuries. Our newspapers, incidentally, are a scandal. A person interested in only one thing will have to buy a huge wad of precious paper to satisfy his or her curiosity – and will throw away nine-tenths of it as being of no interest whatever; and yet trees have been slaughtered to make it all. This is a perfect example of the free workings of the market damaging our planet. They don't always but they do sometimes.

Music. In an ideal world we should make far more of it ourselves, or listen to music made by our neighbours. The country I live in, Ireland, is good in this respect: there is still plenty of fine traditional music and, like so many good things, it is free. We need professional musicians too of course, and composers, and instrument-makers, but all these can operate without damaging the planet.

And the very best things in life for some of us – sitting in the sun, striding over the hills, rowing or sailing on the waters, just being part of and glorying in the unspoilt portions of our planet (and thank God there are a few left) – are free too, or as nearly free as doesn't matter. Virtually any city person can afford a bicycle and, if not, most of us are equipped with a pair of legs on which we can walk. For those unfortunates not so equipped there should be the loving care of people who are.

But we have allowed ourselves to be deluded into thinking that only the things that cost us lots of money can give us pleasure. Nothing *real* pleases us any more. Real life has become so boring to us that we have to turn to television – the lives of the soap stars are so much more exciting and interesting than our own. We can't compete. Where we live is no longer beautiful to us so we are constantly jumping in the car and going somewhere else, seeking what we lack at home and generally not finding it there either. I remember that when I was growing up in the 1920s and '30s the great and constant cry was: 'I'm going to have me a good time!' The good time was everything, and it could only be had with money. That was the *sine qua non*. No good time was to be had without it. Things like sitting quietly under a tree looking out over a lake, or working peacefully in one's garden, or playing with children, or talking to old people, or reading: none of these things came under the heading of 'having me a good time!' And this philosophy of the good time has spread all over the world now, and it is this, as much as anything, that is destroying our planet. Instead of sitting quietly by the lake gazing over it, or rowing a boat on it – which would be good for our souls and our bodies – we must roar about on it in a speed boat, polluting the air, using up scarce petroleum, scaring the birds and making a most abominable noise withal.

The beef barons of Brazil burn the jungle so that they can afford to go to and live it up in Monte Carlo and have themselves, during their lifetimes, a good time. Concern about the welfare of their great grandchildren must not be allowed to interfere with that sacred purpose. It is generally supposed that the peasants of the Third World countries swarm into the city slums simply to search for work and money. My own observation of many of them is that they leave their villages and go there in search of the 'good time'; a thing they are convinced they cannot find in their own homeland. They come to get employment and money too of course but they wouldn't need to if they had fair access to the land at home, and the will to work it.

I have found, as I have watched people over a long life, that the good time just eludes them always. They are not having a good time now but by Jeez they will have one when they get their mitts on enough money. And when they get the money then they must get *more* money. And so nothing must be allowed to interfere with our pursuit of money, nothing. If the world must go down in ruin because of it, then the world is well lost. If we cannot have ourselves a good time then what use is the world anyway?

I knew an old man in Suffolk, a retired farm worker. He always struck me as being the happiest man I had ever met. It may be he was like a dolphin (you can never tell if a dolphin is happy or not because she wears a permanent smile), but my friend's eyes simply sparkled with happiness. He was the very best of company; intelligent, knowledgeable, well read, steeped in the lore of his country and a fine observer of nature too. He could sing, and did, many good songs. I used to meet him at a pub called 'The Nelson' in the village of Ashbocking, just five miles north of the big town of Ipswich. I asked him once about a certain place in Ipswich.

'Ipswich?' he answered, in his lovely Suffolk accent. 'I in't nivver bin there.'

'Never been to Ipswich? But why not?'

'Nivver saw no need. There's everything in the world I need here.' And he beamed me a smile which I, at least, interpreted as being one of pure unalloyed happiness.

There is no instrument, as far as I know, that can measure pleasure, or happiness. It is one thing that economists, for example, cannot include in their calculations, because they have no figures for it. There is a German writer, who uses the pseudonym Tomot Om, who has tried hard to analyse what happiness is. He says that there is a Life Force (which is just his quaint way of saying God; he cannot bring himself to use that now unfashionable three letter word) and that anything that we do which furthers the purpose of the Life Force makes us feel happy while anything that we do which tends to hamper or impede that purpose makes us feel sad. (I can imagine a materialist version of this: anything that increases entropy makes us unhappy; anything that reduces it makes us happy).

So, according to Om's theory, a Brazilian millionaire who causes to be burnt a hundred square miles of Amazon forest to make himself richer cannot be happy, no matter how many gorgeous mistresses he has, or how many villas in the South of France or how many Mercedes Benz. In the pursuit of happiness he is on a hiding to nowhere. I am not claiming that no millionaire can be happy, I am merely claiming that the one I have described can't. Maybe it has something also to do with a camel trying to get through the eye of a needle. Maybe the secret of happiness is that we should always evaluate any course of action that is open to us by thinking (not whether it is pleasing to God as in the old deistic mode of thinking) but whether it is going to damage, or improve, our planet; or, more specifically, the Life which exists on our planet. Will our action make this planet more or less favourable to Life? When we use up non-renewable stored energy we are having a damaging affect on our planet, or at least on our planet's ability to sustain life. We are to a certain extent robbing our posterity. We are increasing entropy – the dispersal and dilution of energy. I am not claiming that we should never use non-renewable energy, I am merely saying that we could consider well before we do. A generation that squanders the natural wealth that it should really share with the generations of the future is like the dissolute squire who gambles away the family estate so that he leaves his children destitute when he dies.

Before young Henry 'jumps in the car' to drive five hundred miles north because he has heard that there is a smattering of snow on the Cairngorms, and he fancies a day's skiing (possibly not because he can't do without it but because it'll be a real piece of one-upmanship to talk about when he gets back to the office) he should think quite seriously what effect his escapade will have on the planet he lives on, and what effect it might have on the lives of his great-great-grandchildren.

In choosing this example I am not condemning skiing. It is a healthy and by itself a completely harmless sport and young Henry may be absolutely besotted with it. And when he considers the worthiness or otherwise of his projected excursion he comes slap up against the Tragedy of the Commons, which we have discussed before in this book. For Henry knows that the pollution that his motorised dash will cause will be as nothing compared to the millions of tons of $CO_2$ and other noxious gases being pumped out by the myriads of other motor vehicles pounding up and down the roads that day. His contribution will be negligible. And of course everybody else thinks like that. All the others are doing it, why should *I* stop?

A trawlerman friend once complained to me about the awful damage that his boat was causing by the practice of beam trawling, which nowadays involves dragging many tons of chain in front of the footrope to plough soles out of the sand. The fishing grounds were being destroyed by it.

'Then why do you *do* it?' I asked.

'Because if I stopped the others would still go on,' he said. 'It wouldn't make a dam' bit of difference if *one* of us stopped. The others would simply get richer and I would get poorer.'

'But if you all go on you will *all* get poorer. You will kill the goose that's laying the golden egg.'

'Well then it should be up to the *government* to stop us.'

Well it should be up to the government to stop the young Henrys of this world from bombing up to the Highlands in their Hondas whenever the spirit moves them. But the government won't. The oil lobby, the road lobby and the car manufacturers' lobby are too strong. Young Henry has got to do it himself. He has got to say: I know I am only one of millions, and my own little tiny contribution makes not a jot of difference to the amount of damage being done; but my own contribution is the only thing that I can control! And therefore I will control it.

So it is up to young Henry himself. He must make his choice of the three scenarios discussed in this book.

If he chooses the Continued Growth Scenario he will go bombing up there in his Honda, flat out, and will not even bother to use unleaded petrol. *And* he will enter his car for the Round Britain Rally next October too.

Or, if he chooses the Palliative Scenario he will go to the Cairngorms in his Honda, but a trifle more slowly, will use unleaded petrol, and will have had a catalytic converter fitted to his exhaust pipe.

But if he chooses the third scenario: the Radical Change one, he will get a fortnight's leave and take the train up to

Pitlochry and, carrying a pup-tent on his back perhaps, will ski-trek over those magnificent mountains and *really* get the feel of the wilderness and refresh his spirit and harden his body, and he will do the world no harm (the train was going anyway) and himself unbounded good, and he will have something worth talking about when he gets back to the office. I have enough confidence in the good sense of young Henry to believe that, when he understands the issues, that is the scenario he will opt for. He will not be a 'Hooray Henry' then, it will be hooray for Henry, and hooray for our old planet too.

And, although the amount of damage saved by Henry's action will be minute, the affects of his decision will spread out like the ripples on a pool: they will be of far greater benefit than the trifling amount of fossil fuel protected or the minuscule reduction in pollution.

The adoption of the Radical Change Scenario, which is the only one that can possibly save our planet, means that each one of us has to take total responsibility for all our actions, without even asking ourselves whether our own tiny contribution will make any difference or not. We are not responsible for what other people do and, except by example and persuasion, we cannot influence them. But we are responsible for what we do. We may or may not believe that we are to be held responsible for our actions in our lives, that we are to be held in some way accountable, but we must believe (because we all know it in our hearts which is really the only way we can know anything) that Nature, or God, or the Life Force – but something, call it what you will – has fitted each one of us with a thing we call a conscience; and it is that that will reward us, or punish us, according to our deserts. We make our own Heaven or Hell.

# Glimpses of the Obvious

---

## Energy

If we burn hydrocarbon fuel we generate $CO_2$.

A carbon-rich atmosphere is good for plants – bad for animals.

We are animals.

If the seas rise it will be good for fish – bad for us.

The most economical machine for turning latent energy into useful work is human muscle.

If there are enough nuclear power stations for long enough there will be nuclear accidents.

With enough nuclear accidents we will all develop cancer.

If fossil fuel-generated power were properly costed it would be found to cost a hell of a lot more than we think it does.

Before we consider generating more power we should see if we can't make do with less of it.

If we continue projecting the curve of human energy requirements upwards it will come to the word EXIT.


## Transport

More roads generate more traffic.

The only cure for traffic problems is less traffic.

If you can't find happiness in your home you won't find it
    in a motor car.


## Trade and Industry

Trade is not necessarily a good thing.
The movement of goods is generally polluting.
Capital-intensive industry causes unemployment.
Labour-intensive industry creates employment.
The less money spent providing each work place in
    industry the less unemployment there will be.
It is only fair that industry should bear the cost of the
    damage it causes to our planet.


## Food and Agriculture

Humans are soil organisms.
If we destroy the soil we will become extinct.
Monoculture always favours disease.
If we put soluble chemicals on the soil some of them will
    end up in our drinking water.
We cannot have agricultural chemicals without having
    agrochemical factories.
Agrochemical factories are always polluting.
It has been demonstrated that we can grow all the food we
    need without the use of agrochemicals.
No pest has been eliminated by pesticides.
Since Life began the animal and vegetable kingdoms have
    been interdependent.
It is wrong to divorce them.

Mechanization of agriculture grows more food per man-hour but *not* more food per acre.

Mechanization always put people out of work.

From soil to mouth, the best road for our food is the shortest.

## Health and Happiness

Health is not a product of the medical industry.

The best way to keep healthy is to keep physically active.

It's also the best way to keep warm.

If our homes are not civilized nothing will be.

There is a limit to the number of people who can inhabit this Earth.

Bigger institutions create bigger problems, but the people who have to solve them remain the same size.

Therefore:

Small is beautiful.